TIME OUT

If anyone comes to Me, listens to My words and obeys them. . . . He is like a man who built a house and dug deep to lay the foundation on rock.

—Luke 6:47, 48 from
Norlie's New Testament

As for yourself, hold fast to what you have
learned and what you know is true, and remember from whom you have learned it. From
your early childhood you have been familiar
with the sacred Scriptures, which can make
you wise to salvation through faith in Christ
Jesus.

—II Timothy 3:14, 15 from
Norlie's New Testament

Foreword

The compiler is indebted to many minds for the contents of *Time Out*, as a glance at the credit lines accompanying the various meditations will soon reveal. Even in the case of the unsigned paragraphs, which are the work of the compiler, he wishes to express his gratitude to many writers who have influenced his thinking and guided his pen in setting these thoughts into words.

These meditations are for the young — in age or spirit, as the case may be. They are not intended for those who feel that they have "arrived" spiritually speaking, but are rather for those who seek daily challenge for their spiritual aspirations. The paragraphs are brief but, it is hoped, will provide ample incentive for meditation throughout the day, encouraging the reader to increase both the quantity and the quality of his quiet time with the Lord.

A word about the new Scripture translations used with many selections in this book. The credit line, "Amplified," which appears frequently, refers to the popular new translation, *The Amplified New Testament,* which is ideal for study and devotional reading because of the fresh clarity it gives to the Scripture. Use of this version, a favorite with young people, is by special permission of The Lockman Foundation, owner of the copyright. *The Berkeley Version of the Holy Bible,* frequently used for Old Testament portions, is also proving valuable in rendering the Scriptures more understandable to today's readers. *Norlie's New Testament* is also quoted and is increasingly popular with today's young people.

T. A. B.

TIME OUT

DAILY DEVOTIONS FOR YOUNG PEOPLE

Compiled and Written by
AL BRYANT
Compiler, *Climbing the Heights*, etc.

ZONDERVAN PUBLISHING HOUSE
GRAND RAPIDS, MICHIGAN

TIME OUT
Copyright 1961 by
Zondervan Publishing House
Grand Rapids, Michigan

First printing . . . . May, 1961
Second printing . . . . . December, 1961
Third printing . . . . June, 1962
Fourth printing . . . . . November, 1962
Fifth printing . . . . April, 1963
Sixth printing . . . . . . December, 1963
Seventh printing . . . . July, 1965
Eighth printing . . . . . November, 1965
Ninth printing . . . . January, 1967
Tenth printing . . . . . . December, 1967
Eleventh printing . . . . . . August, 1968

More than 100,000 copies in print

Printed in the United States of America

TIME OUT

JANUARY

**JAN.
1**
The fear of the Lord is the beginning of wisdom.
—Psalm 111:10

Where we begin determines our destination. We cannot take the road to Chicago and expect to arrive at Detroit. We must begin the Christian life at the only proper point — with a knowledge of God discovered through Jesus Christ. Every other road we take in life must also begin at this point. Every decision must be in the hands of God. Every activity must remain in His will. To understand the meaning of life, we must look at life from God's perspective. We must consider it with His wisdom. That wisdom and that perspective are ours only in Christ. Beginning with Him, this year will be the best and most purposeful we have ever had!

**JAN.
2**
And the people said . . . The Lord our God will we serve and His voice will we obey.
—Joshua 24:24

In the life of everyone there comes a time of decision. It is impossible to spend a lifetime wavering from position to position, never taking a definite stand. Men have tried it, and in so doing have, in effect, made a decision. We might paraphrase the Lord's statement in the New Testament, "he who is not with me, is against me." There is no middle ground, no neutral position, and, notice here, that with decision comes responsibility to follow, to obey. Christians *must* bear fruit. A decision for or against Christ is the most momentous, the supreme decision of life.

He that covereth his sins shall not prosper: but whoso confesseth and forsaketh them shall have mercy.
—Proverbs 28:13

I have seen many young lives start out well after young men and women had trusted Christ as their Saviour. There was a new vigor in their voices, a new sparkle in their eyes, a thrill in their souls all the day long. They loved the prayer meeting. They were fond of Bible study. Spiritual things held a great attraction for them. The battle with Satan was won time after time. Temptations were overcome. There was victory.

Then something happened! It was not noticeable at first except to their close friends. Then everyone began to notice it. There was a lack of interest and a coolness toward spiritual things. Gradually the fire that had once raged in their breasts became only charred embers. The joy and thrill of Christian experience was now a thing of the past. Their lives were powerless and fruitless. They now yielded to temptation; instead of being overcomers they now were overcome. . . . What was wrong? What had made such a radical change as this? Has this been your experience?

The Dakota took off from the Copenhagen airport. Everyone was gay and happy. It was a special event. The passengers included Prince Gustav of Sweden, and Grace Moore, the famous opera singer. Into the air the plane roared — it was a normal routine flight — when suddenly something happened. The nose shot up, the motor stalled and to the horror and amazement of hundreds of spectators, the plane plunged earthward.

An explosion, a flash, and the flight that had started a few moments before ended in tragic horror and death. The world was shocked.

Investigation later proved that a small block on the tail

had not been removed. A ground attendant had been care-less. One little wood block had caused the death of a prince, a world-renowned singer and nineteen other pas-sengers.

One small, tiny, insignificant sin may be the cause of all your difficulty. Confess and forsake. God is plenteous in mercy and will abundantly pardon.   —BILLY GRAHAM

JAN.
4
In the beginning was the Word, and the Word was with God, and the Word was God. —John 1:1

Life is full of beginnings. We are now at the beginning of a year. But here is a beginning that carries our thought back beyond all years, all dates of history, all imaginable periods of time, beyond the beginnings of creation. Then Christ was. What a sublime stretch of being these words give to Him who is our Saviour! We cannot grasp the thought, but we can find security and comfort in it when we think of Christ and when we rest in Him as our hope and salvation. We trust in human friends, and the comfort is very sweet; yet we can never forget that they are but creatures of a day, and that we cannot be sure of having them even for tomorrow. But we trust in Christ, and know that from eternity to eternity He is the same, and therefore our confidence is forever sure and strong.   — J. R. MILLER

JAN.
5
But his wife looked back from behind him, and she became a pillar of salt.   —Genesis 19:26

In the New Testament, Jesus said, "He who puts his hand to the plow, and looks back, is not fit to be one of my disciples." Lot's wife looked back once too often! How can I overcome the temptation of looking back? By fill-ing my days with "looking up." The only path to spiritual progress is forward movement. God makes no allowance for retreat in the spiritual life. Let there be no looking back to things that are past. Like the Apostle Paul, victoriously forge ahead toward God's destination for you!

JAN.
6
When evening came, the owner of the vineyard said to his manager, Call the workmen and pay them their wages, beginning with the last and ending with the first. —Matthew 20:8 Amplified

Jesus used "stories" to illustrate eternal truths. In this parable of the workers in the vineyard, He shows definitely that it is not the length of one's Christian life that counts in eternity — it is the *fact*. Those workmen who had served their Master for a lifetime (from early morning) received no greater wage than those who had served "as by fire." Should this truth discourage a young person from accepting Christ as His Saviour and devoting his life to His service? No, for the rewards of the Christian life begin immediately, even before the enjoyments of eternity. Those rewards alone should be enticement enough. But think of the rest and peace that Christ alone gives. Why risk waiting an eleventh hour call and miss all the blessings that can be yours from the first *through* the eleventh hour? Young person, *now* is the accepted time, *now* is the day of salvation.

JAN.
7
Grace to you, and peace from God our Father, and the Lord Jesus Christ. —Romans 1:7

We are living in such times as never were before. Awful convulsions have shaken the world. Millions have died in recent wars and riots. Thrones have fallen. Sweeping changes have come. Science has now put into man's hands powers of almost unlimited possibility either for racial good or racial destruction. The war-haunted world is a smouldering volcano. It is not strange that apprehensive feelings should cling around us as we peer into the future, and that we fall back with relief on the doctrine of the divine *sovereignty*. Yet somehow even that is not enough. We need the further truth that the God who is sovereign is also "our Father." All our life will feel safer and gladder; the enigmas of human history will assume a kindlier aspect; and the big universe itself will become friendlier, if we go into the new year with this precious truth in mind, that the sovereign God is our Father.

— J. SIDLOW BAXTER

JAN.
8

Behold, God is my salvation; I will trust and not be afraid . . . .   —Isaiah 12:2

It will not save me to know that Christ is a Saviour; but it will save me *to trust* Him to be *my* Saviour. I shall not be delivered from the wrath to come by believing that His atonement is sufficient; but I shall be saved by making that atonement my trust, my refuge, and my all. The pith, the essence of faith lies in this — a casting of oneself on the promise. It is not the life jacket on board ship that saves the man when he is drowning, nor is it his belief that it is an excellent and successful invention. No! He must have it around him, or he will sink.   — SPURGEON

JAN.
9

According to this time it shall be said of Jacob and of Israel, What hath God wrought!
—Numbers 23:23

What will God do in this coming year! Will He, perhaps, jar His sluggish church into long-overdue activity? Will He stir His people out of their lethargy and lassitude? Will there be a revival? If these questions are to be answered in the affirmative, it will mean that something must happen to us as individuals. Revival must begin in the hearts of His people before God will bring about a sweeping change in the world! Let us as young people be willing, yes eager, to lead the way back to God.

JAN.
10

[For my determined purpose is] that I may know Him—that I may progressively become more deeply and intimately acquainted with Him, perceiving and recognizing and understanding [the wonders of His Person] more strongly and more clearly.
—Philippians 3:10 Amplified

At the age of 23, a wise young man of our generation, Jim Elliot, wrote, "Oh the fullness, pleasure, sheer excitement of knowing God on earth. I care not if I ever raise my voice again for Him if only I may love Him, please Him."* If we, with Paul and this young writer, could realize that God and His Son should have our greatest love and devotion, greater even than our desire to serve Him, how much happier our Christian experience would be and how much richer our fellowship with Him. If our first purpose in life is to get to know the Lord better, and better and better — all of the various aspects of our service will fall into their proper place and perspective. Our love for Him, and this is carefully stated that it might not be misunderstood, is more important to Him than our service. It goes without saying that if our hearts are properly attuned to Him, our lives will bear out this fact.

* From *Shadow of the Almighty* by Elisabeth Elliot. Used by permission of the publishers, Harper and Brothers, New York.

JAN.
11

But one thing I do — it is my one aspiration: . . .
— Philippians 3:13 Amplified

Concentration may often be the key to success in a particular endeavor. This is true in modern warfare. If a line of defense can be penetrated at one point, this often wins the battle. In the spiritual sense, concentration is also important. One of Satan's favorite tactics is that of distraction. If he sees one of God's children concentrating on the important issues of life, he does his best to side-track that individual and entice him to direct his efforts toward another goal. With Paul, our purpose should be, ". . . that we may know Him" — that we may have this one aspiration and goal in life, doing His will and accomplishing His purpose.

JAN.
12

When God created man, He made him in God's likeness.
— Genesis 5:1 Berkeley

This is a joyful statement of fact — a simple presentation of a tremendous truth. Since this "birth announcement" was made, many have attempted to "prove" God a liar and man a product of evolution. Time and again men have congratulated themselves on having disproved the Biblical truth of Creation; and time and again the Bible account of creation has withstood the onslaughts of intellectual doubt and aspersions. But, throughout the Word, God has placed gems of lasting truth such as, "We know that, when He [Christ] shall appear, we shall be like Him; for we shall see Him as He is." Thus, God in His divine providence has provided that both the beginning and the end of man will be "in His image and likeness." No matter how often man attacks this citadel of divine strength and provision, the truth still stands unaffected.

JAN.
13
And they were all filled with the Holy Spirit; and they continued to speak the Word of God with freedom and boldness and courage.

—Acts 4:31 Amplified

The man filled with the Holy Spirit has discovered the "fountain of youth." Within his soul are songs never yet sung, music never yet penned, poems never written. There are aspirations not yet realized that pull him on to the hills of eternal life. To the man filled with the Holy Spirit come new visions of God, and new exploits are attempted in the outreach of faith. We follow not a lost cause. We are not engaged in a losing venture. The future is bright with the promises of God for those filled with the Spirit.

—OLIVER G. WILSON

JAN.
14
[Not in your own strength] for it is God Who is all the while effectually at work in you — energizing and creating in you the power and desire — both to will and to work for His good pleasure and satisfaction and delight.—Philippians 2:13 A.N.T.

Finding and following the will of God has always been the key to successful and victorious Christian living. God does not have two ways for His children — He has but one way; not two choices from which His child must make a selection, but one highest and best choice. If your choice is made outside of the will of God, all your effort is wasted, like the useless spinning of a tire on ice or in mud. Only as our effort is directed by and used according to God's will and plan, is God's will and plan carried out. Our supreme desire should be, first of all to discover His will, and secondly, to carry it out in the consciousness that we strive not in our own selves and strength, but in the power and might of Him Whose we are and Whom we serve.

JAN.
15

When he has brought his own sheep outside, he walks on before them, and the sheep follow him, because they know his voice.—John 10:4 Amplified

It was Dr. A. W. Tozer who wrote, "The footprint of the obedient sheep is always found within the larger footprint of the shepherd." This is the key to the Christian life. To get the true picture of what the Lord is presenting here, one must learn that the oriental shepherd dealt with the sheep as individuals. Unlike large scale sheep-herding as we know it in the United States, where the loss of one sheep more or less is of little or no concern, the oriental shepherd knew each of his sheep by name and rather than *driving* them he *led* them as they followed in his footsteps. Knowing that He, the Lord Jesus, goes on before should make our daily walk with Him a blessed one!

JAN.
16

Lo, I am with you all the days — perpetually, uniformly and on every occasion — to the [very] close and consummation of the age.

—Matthew 28:20 Amplified

It is "all the days," not just "always." Isn't it wonderful that the Lord prepares a blessing for each day, coming to us every morning, day after day, and walking with us through our daily situation? Not one of our days is too dull or routine to have His interest and enablement. The fact that we do not realize His presence does not mean He has left us — it simply means that our spiritual eyes are momentarily blinded by the world around us. If we but realize this, our walk will be such that wherever we are He can be our Companion.

JAN.
17

Without having seen Him you love Him; though you do not [even] now see Him you believe in Him, and exult and thrill with inexpressible and glorious (triumphant, heavenly) joy.

—I Peter 1:8 Amplified

The joy of salvation originates in and springs from contact and communion with God. Prayer is the medium of contact and communication. Christian joy is impossible without prayer. It can only be nurtured and sustained by prayer. A prayerless Christian is a joyless Christian. A joyless Christian is a powerless Christian. Powerless Christians make a powerless church. A powerless church results in a sick and decaying society.

G. Campbell Morgan used to tell of a man whose shop had been burned in the great Chicago fire. He arrived at the ruins next morning carrying a table. He set this up amid the charred debris and reared over it the optimistic sign: "Everything lost except wife, children and hope. Business will be resumed as usual tomorrow morning."

The Christian's joy is spontaneous and courageous like this. It is unquenchable and undefeatable and towers above unfavorable circumstances *because it has its source in God.* Communion with the Eternal One taps unfailing resources. Prayerlessness is the first step in joylessness.

—Merrill F. Unger

JAN.
18

And He said to them, Why are you timid and afraid, O you of little faith? —Matthew 8:26
—Amplified

Just before this experience, Jesus had healed the centurion's servant boy and had been greatly pleased and amazed at the man's faith. Now, He is literally shocked at the lack of faith evidenced by His disciples. This is another aspect of the fact of faith. Not only is God limited by our little faith, He is discouraged and disheartened by it. My first purpose as a young person should be to please Him by my faith. My life must be Christ-centered rather than "I" centered. True, *my* strength is small. But equally true, and blessedly so, His strength knows no limitations.

**JAN.
19**

I appeal to you therefore, brethren, and beg of you in view of [all] the mercies of God, to make a decisive dedication of your bodies — presenting all your members and faculties — as a living sacrifice . . . .   Romans 12:1 Amplified

One of the remarkable truths to come out of the tragic martyrdom of the five courageous missionaries who sacrificed their lives at the Auca altar, was the youth of these selfless and devoted men. While still in their late twenties and early thirties, these men had all made their "decisive dedication" and were now called upon to present all on the altar of sacrifice. Almost prophetically, it would seem, one of them, Jim Elliot, at the age of 20 had written, "God, I pray Thee, light these idle sticks of my life and may I burn up for Thee. Consume my life, my God, for it is Thine. I seek not a long life but a full one, like You, Lord Jesus."* What would be accomplished if a whole generation of young people took this attitude toward life?

**JAN.
20**

Rise! traverse the land in its length and its breadth, for to you will I give it. —Genesis 13:17 Berkeley

Spiritually speaking, the land that lies ahead of you is there for the taking, for God has promised that you might "possess the land." These prayer burdens He has laid on

---

* From *Shadow of the Almighty* by Elisabeth Elliot. Used by permission of the publishers, Harper and Brothers, New York.

your heart will be lifted if you move forward in Him. These important decisions which must be made at an early date will resolve themselves if you walk over the land with Him. For He has promised! And not only the prayer burdens and decisions come under His care, but also the responsibilities to witness and to work for Him. That fellow who sits next to you in English class, or the girl across from you in the lab — He will give you wisdom and words to speak to that one about Him. So let's go forward and "possess the land" in confidence and strength.

JAN.
21
Every one who acknowledges Me before men and confesses Me [out of a state of oneness with Me], I will also acknowledge before My Father Who is in heaven . . . . —Matthew 10:32 Amplified

What does it mean to "confess" the Lord Jesus? Basically, confession is nothing more than acknowledgment or admission of a truth. Confession may take the form of "witnessing" as in the case of one testifying in court. Such a one merely tells what he knows, what he has seen and experienced. Opinion is not admissible evidence in court, but fact based on actual experience is. Confession involves more than speech, however — one may confess by the way he lives as well. And if one's life is not constantly guided by what he says, his oral testimony will not "carry much weight." The Christian's responsibility, then, is to always be ready to give a reason, an answer for the faith he has in God through the Lord Jesus. He promises us that if we are outspoken and acknowledge Him as Saviour, He will acknowledge us before God.

JAN.
22

And Jesus increased in wisdom and in stature and years and in favor with God and man.
—Luke 2:52 Amplified

The young person who wants to bring glory to his Heavenly Father must grow spiritually. In order to grow, one must have a willingness to learn and to gain understanding. When King Solomon asked for wisdom that he might rightly rule Israel, God answered him abundantly. And God will honor the sincere prayer of the young person who desires spiritual growth and maturity that he might honor God in his life. Just as in the physical sense, "we are what we eat," so our spiritual growth is controlled by our spiritual diet.

JAN.
23

Give me understanding, and I shall keep thy law . . . .
—Psalm 119:34

The Psalmist here is praying for an illumined understanding, the necessary wisdom to live a consistent Christian life. This is a prayer each of us must raise every day of our lives. We never graduate beyond the grade of dependence upon God for wisdom. The Psalmist goes on to ask, in verse 36, for a "directed" inclination. He asks the Lord to "incline" his heart toward righteousness. He asks, too, for God literally to force him into the paths of righteousness. In verse 35 he says, "Make me" follow the commandments of God. Our prayers should incorporate all of these requests, and our lives should exhibit the fruit of God's work in us.

JAN.
24
Every Scripture is God-breathed — given by His inspiration — and profitable for instruction, for reproof . . . .   —I Timothy 3:16 Amplified

There is such a thing as being "too eager" in our striving toward spiritual "expertness." Many are the warnings in Scripture to "let go and let God" in the matter of spiritual growth. One of the dangers of overeagerness is that we "put words into God's mouth." Some never learn this lesson, but others learn it early in their Christian experience. At the age of 20, Jim Elliot wrote in his diary, "Teach me, Lord, to listen and not always to seek to squeeze truth out of Scriptures which Thou dost not yet choose to open."* Certainly, no one was more zealous to carry out God's will in life than was Jim Elliot, and yet he learned that there is a time to "Be still and know that I am God." One cannot substitute activity for meditation.

JAN.
25
He who is faithful in a very little [thing] is faithful also in much.   —Luke 16:10 Amplified

Thought-provokingly enough, it is often the one with the single talent, the person with the ordinary abilities, who says, "There is so little that I can do, I will not try to do anything." On the other hand, the person with two talents, or five talents, devotes himself wholeheartedly to the work the Lord has given him to do. Thus, it is the ordinary person with average capabilities who often misses life's best — and yet, as Lincoln once said, "God must have loved the common man, for He made so many of them." And it is some of these "common" abilities that make the difference in God's program. If we hide behind our insignificance, we are shunning our responsibilities.

* From *Shadow of the Almighty* by Elisabeth Elliot. Used by permission of the publishers, Harper and Brothers, New York.

**JAN.
26**

For we are God's [own] handiwork (His workmanship), recreated in Christ Jesus, [born anew] that we may do those good works which God predestinated (planned beforehand) for us . . . .
—Ephesians 2:10 Amplified

The ability to live the Christian life is beyond the present strength of the Christian. Isn't it wonderful, then, to know that we are not expected by God to live the Christian life in our own strength? Rather, "we are his workmanship," the possessors of an entirely new source of life, the Lord Jesus Himself. Just as He overcame temptations and obstacles, we, too, in the strength He provides, may live the overcoming life. Our only responsibility is to accept what has been provided, to go ahead on the strength of the promises recorded in the Word.

**JAN.
27**

When thou passest through the waters, I will be with thee; and through the rivers, they shall not overflow thee: when thou walkest through the fire; thou shalt not be burned.   —Isaiah 43:2

This promise does not tell us we shall not need to pass through deep waters, nor does it say we shall not cross turbulent rivers, nor walk in the furnace of affliction. What it does say is that, though those things may come to us, we need not go through them alone. The Great I AM will go with us every step of the way. He measures the depth of the water, the swiftness of the river's current, the intensity of the furnace heat. And His love will not allow the water to be one fraction of an inch deeper than we can pass through. His compassion will not allow the river's current to be one mite stronger than we can stand. His goodness will control the temperature of the furnace so that it will only refine our gold.   — OLIVER G. WILSON

JAN. 28   *Another of the disciples said to Him, Lord, let me first go and bury [care for till death] my father.*
—Matthew 8:21 Amplified

The key to this man's attitude toward Christ is found in the words, "me first." Apparently he was making an excuse for not following Jesus wholeheartedly, for there must have been others at home to care for his father. An older version reveals that he simply said, "Let me first go and bury my father." Yet, his father was not yet dead! So many of our excuses are like this man's — they will not "hold water." May we be true disciples, following after our Master, living wholeheartedly for Him, withholding and reserving nothing for ourselves. We may be assured, from the Word itself, that all of our needs will be supplied, if we put Him first and not *"me!"*

JAN. 29   *Blessed is he who has the God of Jacob for a help, whose hope is in the Lord his God.*
—Psalm 146:5 Berkeley

A more up-to-date word for "blessed" is the often misused, "happy." Happiness is a strong commodity. It seems the more you desire it, the more difficult it is to attain. Landor once said, "We are no longer happy as soon as we wish to be happier." There is much food for thought in this brief but pithy statement. True happiness is a gift — one that must be accepted from the only One who can give it, God Himself. Happiness comes only to those whose God is the Lord, who hope in Him. Happiness is one attribute not gained by trying. Actually, happiness is "learned" by the experience of complete yieldedness and surrender to God, abiding faith and trust in Him.

JAN.
30
Put out into the deep [water] and lower your nets for a haul. —Luke 5:4 Amplified

Decision determines destiny. Many of the uncertainties and perplexities of life would be non-existent if, on the basis of the light given by the Word of God, we would make our decision and proceed with the light we have, leaving the speculation and conjecture which have caused our indecisions. Proceeding thus by faith, we will be surprised at how God's plan unfolds step by step as we go into action. Inaction is unforgivable. Activity, so long as we do not go ahead of God's will, is the divine plan for progress.

JAN.
31
I say unto thee, Arise, and take up thy bed, and go thy way. —Mark 2:11

We have no power in ourselves to do Christ's will, but as we begin to obey, the needed grace is given. Young people often say that they are afraid to enter upon a Christian life because they cannot do what will be required. In their own strength they cannot. It would be as easy for them to climb to the stars as to live unaided a noble and lovely Christian life. Human strength in itself is inadequate to life's sore needs. But the young Christian who sets out in obedience to Christ, depending upon Him to open the path of duty, will never fail of needed help at the moment of need. — J. R. MILLER

FEBRUARY

Then said Jesus unto his disciples, If any man will come after me, let him deny himself, and take up his cross, and follow me. —Matthew 16:24

There is a tendency nowadays to *relax* discipleship. In many Christian sanctuaries the motto is, "Brief, bright, and brotherly." There are sermonettes of fifteen minutes, and Christianettes whose religion costs them nothing but the collection. If there is a meeting between Sundays it is the "Weekly Happy Hour," or the "Pleasant Social Circle," or some other beautifully innocuous rendezvous. The minister must never preach on final retribution or the "wrath to come." Great doctrines such as free grace, election, predestination, regeneration, sanctification, must all be sacrificed to brevity and brightness, while hungry souls starve for lack of Biblical nourishment. — J. SIDLOW BAXTER

But if we have food and clothing, with these we shall be content (satisfied). —I Timothy 6:8
—Amplified

A word of wisdom from James Scott bears out Paul's discernment in the verse above. Scott summed it all up when he said, "No man is so sad as he who has much and wants more." This is strikingly true and indicative of the "hurry-scurry" philosophy of today. It seems that the more people have in the way of material things, the more frustrated they become in the mad rush to gain more. As Christians, we can find complete satisfaction when our barest necessities are supplied, for we have the hope and the promise of an eternity where *every* desire of our hearts will find satisfaction in Christ.

FEB.
3

I press on toward the goal to win the [supreme and heavenly] prize to which God in Christ Jesus is calling us upward. —Philippians 3:14 Amplified

One of the most discerning evaluations of the Christian life was made by martyred Jim Elliot at the age of 22. He wrote, "One of the great blessings of Heaven is the appreciation of Heaven on earth. *He is no fool who gives what he cannot keep to gain what he cannot lose.*"* This young man had learned the same lesson as the Apostle Paul. The goal of life is eternal life, not the empty rewards of earth. Thus, earthly life for its own sake becomes value-less and purposeless. On the other hand, if life is lived with eternity's values in view, life takes on a whole new aura of meaning, a whole new area of purpose. Paul also wrote, "The preaching of the cross is to them that perish, foolishness," a truly discerning evaluation. But to us who believe, "It is the power of God unto salvation."

FEB.
4

And He (God) said: Take now thy son, thine only son Isaac . . . and offer him there for a burnt offering . . . . —Genesis 22:2

Our Heavenly Father is not as much interested in the *quantity* of our devotion to Him as He is in the *quality* of our love. Abraham could have sacrificed a calf or a lamb and not even missed it, but what kind of love would that have expressed? How deep would his devotion have been if expressed as lightly as that? No, God wants our very best, our most prized possession. If I give Him part of myself, but reserve a portion for my own personal pleasures, I have not measured up to His standard, for He gave His best for me.

* From *Shadow of the Almighty* by Elisabeth Elliot. Used by permission of the publishers, Harper and Brothers, New York.

FEB.
5
. . . Striving side by side and *contending with a single mind for the faith of the glad tidings.*
—Philippians 1:27 Amplified

Our business in life is not to get ahead of other people, but to get ahead of ourselves. To break our own record; to outstrip our yesterdays by todays; to bear our trials more beautifully than we ever dreamed we could; to whip the tempter inside and out as we never whipped him before; to give as we never have given; to do our work with more force and a finer finish than ever; to get ahead of ourselves — that is the true idea. To beat some one else in a game, or to be beaten, may mean much or little. To beat ourselves means a great deal. Whether we win or not, we are playing better than we ever did before, and that's the point after all — to play better the game of life.
— M. D. BABCOCK

FEB.
6
Christ liveth in me.
—Galatians 2:20

Scientists tell of certain birds which in their wild state do not sing, but which have in their throats fine muscles, showing that if they had grown up in a favorable environment they might have been good singers. There is no one who has not more life muscles than he has learned to use. We have capacities for obedience, for service, for beautiful living, for usefulness which lie undeveloped in us. Instead of letting ourselves slacken in the doing of our duty, we should ever set ourselves a higher work, and every day add a line to the quality of our life and the worthiness of our character.
— J. R. MILLER

FEB.
7

For I know nothing by myself; yet am I not hereby justified: but he that judgest me is the Lord.
—I Corinthians 4:4

The American humorist, Josh Billings, once said, "It is better to know nothing than to know what ain't so." Seriously, perhaps Paul had somewhat of this philosophy in mind as he wrote to the Corinthians. Paul made no claims for his own knowledge, but gave all the credit to God, looking to the Lord for wisdom and understanding. Paul must have kept an "open mind" on spiritual matters, so that the Lord could speak to him and show him spiritual truth. We, as Christian young people, should do the same, conscious of our needs and shortcomings as children of God.

FEB.
8

O Lord, thou has searched me, and known me . . . and art acquainted with all my ways.
—Psalm 139:1, 3

Each time something frightening floats to the surface of my subconscious mind and registers its ugly self on my consciousness, I deliberately remind myself that God is not shocked by the things I am just now seeing about me. "While we were yet sinners, Christ died for us." He is *unshockable* and *unshakable,* and He is, in the Person of the blessed Holy Spirit, *constantly* at work in the shadowy depths of our subconscious minds. This is His domain if we are Christians. Here we have no control. And even when consciously we feel out of touch with God, we can absolutely *rest* on the fact that *He* is *not* out of touch with us. He is there in the depths right now working.
— Eugenia Price

FEB.
9

No longer be children, tossed [like ships] to and fro between chance gusts of teaching, and wavering with every changing wind of doctrine . . . . Rather . . . grow up in every way and in all things into Him . . . . —Ephesians 4:14, 15 Amplified

A wise man once said, "Ideas are like beards: men do not have them until they grow up." This is particularly true in the spiritual realm. One who is yet a "babe in Christ" has not reached the point in his spiritual growth when he can, as it were, begin having independent ideas of his own on spiritual matters. But, he should seek to grow in grace and in the knowledge of the Lord Jesus Christ so that he may begin, spiritually speaking, to stand on his own two feet.

FEB.
10

O God, thou art my God; early will I seek thee . . . . —Psalm 63:1

Touching God is like touching a live wire. He sends power through our whole being. Any one can touch a dead wire and never be different, or never know that he touched it. No one, however, can touch God and be unmoved. We cry as Isaiah of old, "Woe is me for I am undone, for mine eyes have seen Jehovah of Hosts." To meet God thus in our morning watch assures us a day of gracious ministry for others. We need more of God in our lives, more of His purity, more of His love, more of His grace, more of His strength. If all our spiritual help and resources lie in Him, if He is the source and fountain of all blessing and benediction, then our first and foremost care ought to be to meet Him alone in the morning hour.

— MERRILL F. UNGER

FEB.
11
And behold, they brought to Him a man paralyzed and prostrated by illness, lying on a sleeping pad, and when Jesus saw their faith He said . . . your sins are forgiven . . . . —Matthew 9:2 Amplified

The heart of Jesus was warmed by the faith these men revealed in behalf of their friend. This is another aspect of faith — unselfishness. Our faith should be not only large, but also "other-centered," in a sense at least. We should not lavish all of our "spiritual means" on ourselves, but we should spend some on others. My concern for others should so grip me that my own spiirtual problems will be minimized as I seek to help others. That is what happened to these men who brought their paralyzed friend to Jesus.

FEB.
12
Righteousness exalts a nation, but sin is a reproach to any people. —Proverbs 14:34 Berkeley

Today is the birthday of one of the greatest Americans who ever lived — Abraham Lincoln. Yet Lincoln was a very humble man, not seeking greatness but finding it because of his out-spoken reliance upon God. In the crisis periods of his life, he turned to God for guidance and counsel. His deep faith in God and the Word was revealed time and again during his term as president. And he has left our country a spiritual heritage which seems to grow with every passing year. As long as Lincoln is remembered and revered, this country will have, at its heart, the right relationship to God. If the day ever comes, however, when this country turns its back upon Lincoln and his God, history will record the downfall of a once mighty nation. Righteousness must be the motto of our great nation.

And whoever gives to one of these little ones [in rank or influence] even a cup of cold water because he is My disciple, surely, I declare to you, he shall not lose his reward. —Matthew 10:42
—Amplified

What is involved in "discipleship," the act of "following after" the Lord Jesus? Is it possible to be a born-again Christian and not a wholehearted follower? These are questions which have plagued the Church of Jesus Christ down through the centuries, questions which are particularly troublesome to young people. The Word Itself has the answer, and Jesus here defines practical Christianity. In another place Jesus says, "By their fruit ye shall know them," meaning that the fruits of a tree — and a Christian — are the most reliable measure of the true nature of the tree — and the Christian.

Being confident of this very thing, that he which hath begun a good work in you will perform it.
—Philippians 1:6

If any sincere Christian cast himself with his whole will upon the Divine Presence which dwells within him, he shall be kept safe unto the end. What is it that makes us unable to persevere? Is it want of strength? By no means. We have with us the strength of the Holy Spirit. It was not that strength failed the will, but that the will failed first. If we could but embrace the Divine will with our whole love, cleaving to it and holding fast by it, we should be borne along as upon "the river of the water of life." We open only certain chambers of our will to the influence of the Divine will. We are afraid of being wholly absorbed into it. And yet, if we would have peace, we must be altogether united to Him.   — H. E. Manning

FEB.
15
No man can serve two masters. . . . Ye cannot
serve God and mammon. —Luke 16:13

Opposed to the single eye and the unity of life that it brings is the divided life — the hopeless effort to serve two masters. Christ does not mean that we cannot *have* two masters (that one cannot be clerk in a bank and a follower of Christ as well) but, that we cannot serve two masters — in the sense that we cannot have two controlling and ultimate loyalties as different as God and mammon. We can have many different purposes and loyalties provided they are all grouped around God or around mammon. But one central focus they must have, one final authority there must be; and if it is God, it cannot be mammon. In the last analysis one has to give way.

— J. T. Addison

FEB.
16
Then He said to the man, Reach out your hand.
And the man reached it out, and it was restored. . . .
—Matthew 12:13 Amplified

Here is a true illustration of what "salvation" is. What this man could not do for himself, God through the Lord Jesus Christ accomplished. The man's only responsibility was to obey the command, "reach out your hand." The sinner's only responsibility, in the transaction we call salvation, is to "reach out" and take the hand God has extended. Ours is a need that only Christ can satisfy. We cannot merit His help — we can simply accept it. If we are to be "restored" to the original sinless contact with God, the Creator, that Adam enjoyed before the fall, we must willingly cast ourselves upon His mercy, acknowledging our need and our own emptiness, accepting His restoring ability and capability. Yield your life to Him as this man gave his infirmity and enjoyed restoration.

FEB.
17

To the centurion Jesus said, Go; it shall be done for you as you have believed. And the servant boy was restored to health at that very moment.
—Matthew 8:13 Amplified

Could it be that small faith limits God? What if the Roman soldier in the verse for today had not had great faith in the ability of Christ to restore his servant? This is a thought-provoking question — a question that will not be answered this side of eternity. Yet, in a way, the question has been answered in the lives and experiences of countless Christians down through the ages. Those who have accomplished much, spiritually speaking, those who have truly lived by faith, have proved, to a degree at least, that blessings are tailored to our faith. Great faith — great blessing. Little faith — little blessing. Live this day faithfully and well, in the realization that God is our Faith and wants to bless us abundantly — if there is nothing in our lives to hinder Him.

FEB.
18

The Lord hath been mindful of us, He will bless us . . . but we will bless the Lord from this time forth and for evermore. Praise the Lord.
—Psalm 115:12-18

No one else is worthy of our praise, except the one who made us and sustains us. It is wonderful that our God is "mindful of us" and "will bless us." Not because of what we are, but because of who He is. In the light of this promise, how carefree and fearless we should be. As we think back upon His blessings and look ahead to His promises for the future, His praise should be continually on our lips. As we praise Him it seems that our blessings become even greater. As we acknowledge His greatness, it seems that we become more willing to be led by Him.

FEB.

19

But the earth had grown corrupted in God's sight; the earth was filled with lust for power . . . and (was) . . . degenerated. . . . All those living on the earth had perverted their way.

—Genesis 6:11, 12 Berkeley

The account of the condition of the world in Noah's day is strangely reminiscent of conditions that prevail today. But Noah found favor in the presence of the Lord, in spite of the evilness of his generation. That, too, should be true of Christians today. In contrast to worldly excesses in every area of life, the Christian young person should be characterized by a godly, circumspect walk, one which by its very conduct reveals the difference between the good and the evil, the Christ-like and the Satanic.

FEB.

20

God said, I will dwell in and with and among them. . . . —II Corinthians 6:16 Amplified

We read in a British publication about a young German doctor, now an earnest Christian but once a member of Hitler Youth and a soldier in Hitler's army, who, speaking in a British church, said: "I am concerned with the casual quality of the faith of youth. You do not give to Christ anything like the devotion which German youth once gave to Hitler."

"God hath said, I will dwell in them and walk in them; and I will be their God, and they shall be my people." Such dignity and honor conferred upon us cause the soul to bow low in humiliation at the foot of the Cross. If we are the temple of the living God, we must be holy. We must submit our will to God's will. We must strive to live daily as pleases Him and as becomes holiness.

— OLIVER G. WILSON

FEB.
21
Thou has set our iniquities before thee, our secret sins in the light of thy countenance. —Psalm 90:8

A single sin, however apparently trifling, however hidden in some obscure corner of our consciousness — a sin which we do not intend to renounce — is enough to render real prayer impracticable. A course of action not wholly upright and honorable, feelings not entirely kind and loving, habits not spotlessly chaste and temperate — any of these are impassable obstacles. If we know of a kind act which we might, but do not intend to, perform, if we be aware that our moral health requires the abandonment of some pleasure which as yet we do not intend to abandon, here is cause enough for the loss of all spiritual power.

— F. B. Cobbe

FEB.
22
And whatsoever ye do, do it heartily, as to the Lord, and not unto men. —Colossians 3:23

Religion is not one department of life. It is the whole of life. Church-going and church activity are of course not the whole of life; even praying and reading the Bible are not the whole of life. Religion is far deeper and wider than these varied aspects. Our "religion" is the name for our relation to God through Christ and to all our fellows through Christ. It is not a particular set of ideas or of actions that applies in one field and not in others. It is a fellowship with God and men that stands fast and holds good wherever we turn and whatever we do. It *is* the whole of life because it colors and interprets the whole of life. If we do not take religion seriously it becomes a mere compartment of life. But if we do take it seriously it becomes the central dynamo of life. — J. T. Addison

FEB.
23
And he (Abraham) looked toward Sodom and Gomorrah . . . and lo, the smoke of the country went up as the smoke of a furnace. — Genesis 19:28

To this day Sodom and Gomorrah are not shown on any map of the Holy Land. In fact, so-called higher critics have questioned that such cities ever existed. Archeologists have found, however, a thick layer of salt near the Dead Sea, under which Sodom is believed to be buried — another scientific proof of the Bible's authenticity and authority. Once again, God has proved Himself faithful to His Word and promise. God not only promises good to His children, but He also promises the just reward for wickedness. The same God who said, "Be sure your sins will find you out," also loved the world so much that He gave His only begotten Son, that those who believed might be saved. Take God at His Word.

FEB.
24
And be not conformed to this present age, but be ye transformed by the renewing of your mind that ye may prove what is that good and acceptable and perfect will of God. —Romans 12:2

God would have our lives so yielded to Him that there shall be no artificial separation between the sacred and the secular. He would have everything marked, "holiness unto the Lord" (Zechariah 14:20). We must take Him into our business as well as into our pleasure. We must be able to take Him with us where we go on Saturday night as well as with us to church on Sunday morning. This can only be accomplished as we obey the injunction, "keep filled with the Spirit," and as a result of this inner tide of spiritual power, we shall "walk in the Spirit." May the Spirit Himself work this happy condition in our hearts!
— MERRILL F. UNGER

**FEB.
25**

In Him we live, and move, and have our being.
—Acts 17:28

Where then is *our* God? You say, He is *everywhere:* then show me *anywhere* that you have met Him. You declare Him *everlasting:* then tell me *any moment* that He has been with you. You believe Him ready to help them that are tempted, and to lift those that are bowed down: then in what passionate hour did you subside into His calm grace? in what sorrow did you lose yourself in His "more exceeding" joy? These are the testing questions by which we may learn whether we too have raised our altar to an "unknown God" and worship as the blind; or whether we really walk with Him "in whom we live, and move, and have our being."

— J. MARTINEAU

**FEB.
26**

And whoever falls on this Stone will be broken to pieces, but he on whom it falls will be crushed to powder, and it will winnow him, scattering him as dust.
—Matthew 21:44 Amplified

Not many would dare to pray, as Jim Elliot did at the age of 20, "Father, make of me a crisis man. Bring those I contact to decision. Let me not be a milepost on a single road; make me a fork that men must turn one way or another on facing Christ in me."* This is a daring prayer, one which only a completely dedicated man could afford to pray. If there were more "Christian crisis men," the message of the Gospel and the work of the Church would certainly be more widespread and effective. The failure is not with God. The failure is with men.

* From *Shadow of the Almighty* by Elisabeth Elliot. Used by permission of the publishers, Harper and Brothers, New York.

**FEB.
27**

And in every work that he began in the service of the house of God, and in the law, and in the commandments, to seek his God, he did it with all his heart, and prospered. —II Chronicles 31:21

God is a kind Father. He sets us all in the places where He wishes us to be employed; and that employment is truly "our Father's business." He chooses work for every creature which will be delightful to them, if they do it simply and humbly. He gives us always strength enough, and sense enough, for what He wants us to do. —F. B. MEYER

**FEB.
28**

Bear ye one another's burdens, and so fulfil the law of Christ. —Galatians 6:2

Let us remember that God's call comes to us most often and most continuously through the needs of men . . . . Every burden we help to bear will prove us in partnership with Him who is ever calling men to roll their burdens on Him. — G. CAMPBELL MORGAN

**FEB.
29**

The horse is made ready for the day of battle, but the victory belongs to the Lord.
—Proverbs 21:31 Berkeley

One who has this philosophy of life will not be troubled with pangs of anxiety. A wise man of old once said, "An optimist sees an opportunity in every calamity, a pessimist a calamity in every opportunity." Undoubtedly, the optimist would believe the entire verse quoted above — but the pessimist would find himself defeated at the mere thought of the battle mentioned in the middle of the verse. As Christian young people, ours is the blessed assurance that "the victory belongs to the Lord" indeed!

MARCH

MARCH 1   *Vexation slays the fool, and jealousy kills the simple.*
—Job 5:2 Berkeley

One of the early church fathers, Chrysostom, once commented, "As a moth gnaws a garment, so does envy consume a man." The temptation to be envious of others is one of the most subtle pitfalls into which a man, be he believer or unbeliever, can fall, a problem many Christian people must face. And this jealousy can be as destructive and annihilating as a full-fledged attack on a woolen garment by a cloud of moths. How does one overcome this natural human tendency? In verse 8 of Job 5, Job's friend, Eliphaz admonishes, ". . . as for me, I would seek God and I would commit my cause to God. . . ." The secret of victory over this temptation, then, is to yield it along with all of our other problems to our all-powerful God.

MARCH 2   *Stop being perpetually uneasy (anxious and worried) about your life. . . .*—Matthew 6:25 Amplified

Peace of mind is the object most universally sought in the world today, even by young people. Many, after exhausting themselves in fruitless search, have ended life in a mental institution or as a suicide. Thousands of years ago, Philosopher Seneca observed, "The mind that is anxious about the future is miserable." The only adequate solution to this anxiety is found in the admonition of Jesus recorded above. As soon as we have shifted our anxiety, along with our sins, to the waiting shoulder of our Saviour, we have set out on the path of perfect peace and quiet contentment, for our future is assured in His hands.

MARCH 3

He who is not with Me (definitely on My side), is against Me, and he who does not (definitely) gather with Me and for My side, scatters.
—Matthew 12:30 Amplified

The Apostle James refers to this condition of heart and mind as "double mindedness" and the Lord Himself once warned that a house divided against itself cannot stand. What is true of houses or kingdoms is also strikingly and graphically true of the mind. Double-mindedness is something like traveling the wrong way down a one way street. And just as surely as it leads to trouble and disaster in the physical realm, so it does in the spiritual realm as well. There can be no neutrality, no neutral position, with regard to our attitude toward God. Unless our love for Him is complete, encompassing all of us, our spiritual lives will be doomed to failure and halfway accomplishment.

MARCH 4

Peace I leave with you, my peace I give unto you: not as the world giveth, give I unto you. Let not your heart be troubled, neither let it be afraid.
—John 14:27

Young people everywhere come to me and say, "If I become a Christian I will have to give up so much. You can't have a good time and be a Christian." Listen, young people, you do not begin to live until you know Christ. The young people around the world today who are having the best time are the young people who know Jesus Christ as their Saviour. They know what real living is. I have heard the hollow, shallow laughter of the world. I have heard the genuine laughter of the beaming young Christian. I know there is a difference. — BILLY GRAHAM

MARCH 5

For by your words you will be justified and acquitted, by your words you will be condemned and sentenced. —Matthew 12:37 Amplified

The modern-day cardiograph seems almost miraculous in its ability to reveal the inmost secrets of the human heart — the physical secrets, that is. But 2000 years ago Jesus described a more accurate cardiograph for revealing the heart's spiritual secrets — and He said that this spiritual cardiograph was so accurate that it could be relied upon as evidence in court, for out of the fulness, the superabundance of the heart, the mouth speaks. No more accurate "X-ray of the heart" could be made. Remember that your words are a cardiograph, revealing your heart's innermost secrets to all those around you — in school, at work, or wherever you are.

MARCH 6

Do not lay hands on the lad, (God) said, do nothing to him. —Genesis 22:12 Berkeley

Speaking from a purely human viewpoint, it would seem that God was fickle and temperamental in His dealings with Abraham and the sacrifice of Isaac. One minute He said, "Do it" and the next, "Don't do it!" But what about the lesson Abraham learned in this experience? What about the faithful obedience he showed, not only here but in other events of his life? No, God is not fickle or temperamental — He is all seeing and all knowing, the only One adequate to test and try man — the only One of high enough caliber to "train" His children for the army of the Lord. If you as a young person are called upon to undergo testing, be thankful for this evidence of God's interest in you and His love for your eternal soul.

MARCH 7

Who shall deliver me from the body of this death?
—Romans 7:24, 25

What is sin? This chapter is a great story of a tragedy, the awful power of sin. The suggestions that it is an infirmity, a form of heredity, or mere selfishness do not satisfy the soul's real sense of guilt, however plausible they are as theories. They all leave God out of the picture. We may excuse others, but we cannot lighten our own sense of responsibility. It is revolt against God and it leads to loss of life. Education and environment will not remove its power; they may only change the place of emphasis. I thank God through Jesus Christ. Christ did not come to describe sin but to destroy it.   — J. H. JOWETT

MARCH 8

But I am like a green olive tree in the house of God.
—Psalm 52:8

The olive is crushed into oil, and the oil is used for smoothing and supplying joints and flesh, for nourishing and sustaining the body as food, for illuminating darkness as oil in the lamp. And these three things are the things for which we Christian people have received all our gentleness, and all our beauty, and all our strength — that we may give other people light, that we may be the means of conveying to other people nourishment, that we may move gently in the world as lubricating, sweetening, soothing influences — not irritating or provoking, not leading to strife or alienation. The question, after all, is this: Does anybody gather fruit off us, and would anybody call us "trees of righteousness, the planting of the Lord, that He may be glorified"? May we all open our hearts for the dew from heaven, and then use it to produce in ourselves . . . fruitfulness!   — ALEXANDER MACLAREN

MARCH 9 *Ephraim, he hath mixed himself among the people; Ephraim is a cake not turned.* —Hosea 7:8

One wonders if the Lord may have been thinking of Ephraim when He said, "Seek ye first the kingdom of God, and all these things will be added to unto you." It is certainly true that divided loyalties merely serve to "water down" our witness. Christians cannot be a "mixture"; they must be undiluted — and undeluded as well. Certainly with the authoritative Textbook the Christian has in the Bible and the power he has in Christ, he should be the most effective witness and worker the world has ever seen.

MARCH 10 *Now faith is the assurance (the confirmation, the title-deed) of the things [we] hope for, being the proof of things [we] do not see and the conviction of their reality.* —Hebrews 11:1 Amplified

There is an excellent example of faith in one of today's most common actions — the dropping of a letter into a mail box. Faith, with assurance, drops its letter and lets it go. Distrust, on the other hand, holds on to a corner of the letter and wonders why the answer never comes. A letter must be entrusted to the post office to accomplish its purpose.

MARCH 11 *If a person [really] loves Me, he will obey My word.* —John 14:23 Amplified

As Christians we often get "the cart before the horse" in the matter of serving the Lord. We earnestly pray that God would use us, forgetting to pray that we might be, first of all, in the center of His will, and that we might live up to His standards. If we could only realize how much our disobedience can hinder God, we would recognize the importance of complete conformity to God's will.

MARCH 12   *. . . strait is the gate, and narrow is the way, which leadeth unto life, and few there be that find it.*
—Matthew 7:14

A bee-keeper told the story of a hive — how, when the little bee is in the first stage of growth, it is put into a hexagonal cell, and honey enough is stored there for its use until it reaches maturity. The honey is sealed in with a capsule of wax, and when the tiny bee has fed itself on the honey and exhausted the supply, the time has come for it to emerge into the open. But oh, the wrestle, the tussle, the straining to get through the wax! It is the straight gate for the bee, so straight that in the agony of exit the bee rubs off the membrane that hid his wings, and when he reaches the other side he is able to fly!

— JOHN ROBERTS

MARCH 13   *Abraham then reached out his hand and took hold of the knife to slay his son.*
—Genesis 22:10 Berkeley

This was true obedience on Abraham's part — obedience to a command of God which must have seemed to him senseless and fruitless. How absurd to kill the son of promise before the promise was fulfilled! But faithful Abraham does not question God's authority. If he had been obedient only to the point of binding Isaac to the altar, that would not have been obedience at all. Abraham must be willing to lift the knife and plunge it into his beloved son's heart — that is the only kind of obedience acceptable to God. How often my so-called "obedience" must chafe the Heavenly Father — by not being sincere at all!

MARCH 14

And no man is able to pluck them out of My Father's hand.
—John 10:29

God is superior to the slum or the tenement, to ungodly companions or influence. God is greater than the sneer of the mocker. Live in God consciously, and you have found the environment that is highest and closest and strongest, the environment which is superior to all others. — MORGAN

MARCH 15

The spirit is willing, but the flesh is weak.
—Matthew 26:41

Tell God that you are willing to be made willing about all. A lady was once in great difficulties about certain things which she felt eager to keep under her own control. Her friend, hoping to encourage her into the better life of consecration, placed before her a blank sheet of paper, and urged her to write her name at the foot, and then to lay it before God in prayer. She did so, and at once entered this blessed life. Are you willing to do this? Are you prepared to sign your name to a blank sheet of paper and then hand it over to God, for Him to fill in as He pleases? If not, ask Him to make you willing and able to do this and all things else. You never will be happy until you let the Lord Jesus keep the house of your nature, closely scrutinizing every visitor and admitting only His friends. He must reign. He must have all or none. He must have the key of every closet, of every cupboard, and of every room. Do not try to make them fit for Him. Simply give Him the key. And He will cleanse and renovate and make beautiful.
— F. B. MEYER

MARCH 16

Things began to happen before he had done speaking. —Genesis 24:15 Berkeley

Abraham's old and trusted servant knew the God of his master Abraham, and *specifically* prayed for guidance in the finding of a wife for Isaac. And the Bible tells us, "Things began to happen before he had done speaking. . . ." How illustrative of God's ability and desire to answer prayer! For the young person, prayer should certainly play a prominent part, not only in the search for a life's mate, but in the conduct of the home ultimately established. And we as young people should not be afraid to be specific, for God delights to give specific answers to specific requests.

MARCH 17

The rulers . . . derided him, saying, he saved others; let him save himself, if he be Christ. —Luke 23:35

During a plague in Marseilles, the physicians decided that nothing could be done to save the people unless a victim could be dissected, and the nature of the disease thus learned. But who would do such a perilous work? One physician arose and said he would do it. Saying farewell to his family he entered the hospital, made the dissection, wrote out the results, and in a few hours was dead. But now the physicians could treat the disease, and the plague was stayed.

These incidents illustrate Christ's devotion to death for sinners. Men could not be saved unless some one could suffer and die in their room, and Jesus became the propitiation for sins. In one sense He could have saved Himself, but then the world would have been lost. His death was voluntary. He gave His life for the sheep. We are saved because He saved not Himself.   — J. R. MILLER

MARCH 18 *The Lord knoweth the way of the righteous: but the way of the ungodly shall perish* —Psalm 1:6

Have you ever seen how a road "breaks up" in the spring after a hard winter? But have you noticed how certain stretches of road never seem to be disturbed by the changing seasons? That is the difference between a "good" and a "bad" road. That is the way it is with the ungodly. Their road is a poorly prepared one. Its very foundations are rotten, built of "wood, hay and stubble." But Christ said, "I am the way!" And that is the good road, the road whose builder and maker is God. Changing circumstances cannot affect its condition, for it remains the only perfectly prepared way, a way down which young and old may walk side by side in equal peace and happiness.

MARCH 19 *Whoever will humble himself therefore, and becomes [trusting, lowly, loving, forgiving] as this little child, is greatest in the kingdom of heaven.* —Matthew 18:4 Amplified

Humility is an often overlooked virtue of the Christian life. Please notice, however, that it comes as an act of the *will* of the Christian. Humility is not a gift of God as salvation is. I must humble myself by a conscious act of my will. Young people are as susceptible to pride as those of any age, and because they are susceptible, must be always on the alert for the subtle progress of pride in their lives. While God does not hand humility to us "on a silver platter," He does provide ample strength to overcome it if we will yield ourselves to Him. Remember, too, that humility does not connote spinelessness or cowardice. Humility is merely living in the consciousness of your own unworthiness in the light of His righteousness — living a life pleasing to Him because it is yielded to Him.

We often hear these words quoted, usually with the meaning that whether a man is high or low, rich or poor, it makes no difference to God. The principle is generally applied to social distinctions, and on that point we are all agreed. But St. Paul's great utterance first applied to races. He declares that no racial distinctions have any importance in the sight of God; no differences but moral differences are vital in His sight. God is equally interested in the Jew and in the Gentile. And likewise, we may add, He is equally interested in the Hindu, in the American, and in the Filipino. That sounds simple; but it is a staggering piece of news to most "Nordics," for we can hardly grasp the amazing thought that all the hundreds of millions of yellow and black men are just as well known to God as we and quite as interesting. We think of them in the mass at a distance and find them too numerous to know and too far away to matter. But He knows each one of them from within as individuals. — J. T. ADDISON

There is a conditional aspect to God's guidance — that is, that I be "on the way." It would be foolish to expect the Lord to lead me along a way which I did not desire to follow, a way in which I was not already standing, a direction in which my face was not already turned. This is a good illustration of what "conversion" is — a turning into the way which God would have me to go — a willingness to allow Him to lead me in that way. Do not expect God's guidance unless you are already in His way.

MARCH 22 *Not one of them (a sparrow) will fall to the ground without your Father's leave and notice.*
—Matthew 10:29 Amplified

The door of our garage was left partly open. A sick sparrow crept in and at one side, behind a bundle of newspapers, the sick little sparrow died alone — no, it was not alone, God was there. G. Campbell Morgan says of this passage: "Do not spoil this quotation by saying that Jesus meant that not one of them shall fall to the ground without the Father's knowledge. He did not say that. The King said that God is with the dying sparrow." I felt a sense of awe as I carried the dead sparrow to a place of burial — God was present. Jesus is showing that the smallest details of life are in God's knowledge and under His matchless care. He who feeds the sparrow will not starve the saint. Nothing can come to the trusting child of God except as God permits it. From the dungeon comes a *Pilgrim's Progress* and from the hours of perpetual darkness comes the soul-inspiring music of a Fanny Crosby.

— OLIVER G. WILSON

MARCH 23 *And they were deeply and exceedingly grieved and distressed.*
—Matthew 17:23 Amplified

Jesus' disciples had just heard plainly from His lips that He was on the threshold of death, but that He would be victorious over it. So concerned were they with His coming suffering and death, that they apparently overlooked the glorious victory which would result from His sacrificial death and redemptive resurrection. It is easy for all of us to become so involved in the so-called "tragedies" of life that we do not even see the "triumphs."

MARCH 24 *Blessed is the man that trusteth in the Lord, and whose hope the Lord is.* —Jeremiah 17:7

If you want to know something about hope, real hope, talk to a man who is trusting the Lord. What a thing it is to have hope in a day like this! The best part of all is, if you are living without this hope, it is not too late. "If any man hear my voice, and open the door, I will come in to him" — that is Christ speaking to you even this day. You may say, "Come in," or you may decide to go on the way you're going. Choose we all must, and often the battle is terrible. The world seems to offer much. Satan's greatest achievement is to blind our eyes and make us think that outside of Christ is real living. It is only after we have chosen Christ that our eyes are opened to the riches of His glory.

It is a great and glorious thing to be a Christian, and so hopeful! I shall never quite get over it. Christ in me — my hope of glory; and besides all that, Christ is putting eagle wings on my earthly hopes. — BETTY CARLSON

MARCH 25 *The Lord hath need of him.* —Mark 11:3

There seems to have been no formal request of the owner for the use of the colt. Jesus sent His disciples to take it by Divine authority. So then the Lord has a right to anything we have. No property right that we can get takes the title out of His hands. We talk about our possessions as if they were ours indeed. Nothing is really ours save as lent to us by the Lord to be used for Him.

— J. R. MILLER

MARCH 26 *God is a Spirit [a spiritual Being] and those who worship Him must worship Him in spirit and in truth (reality).* —John 4:24 Amplified

What does it mean to worship in Spirit? Should I interpret this verse to mean it is unnecessary to worship in the presence of others? Does this verse mean that I do not need church membership to worship completely? In a sense, a child of God may worship anywhere. Worship is an attitude of heart, not a place. But, just as I must depend on others, in a sense, for physical food, I must also depend upon others for a well-rounded spiritual diet. There are times when I can worship in solitude, perhaps surrounded by nature's beauty. But I will miss much of the blessing of communion with God if I never share this blessing with fellow Christians.

MARCH 27 *What time I am afraid, I will trust in Thee.* —Psalm 56:3

The great man of prayer, George Mueller, was once asked the secret of strong faith. "The only way to learn strong faith," replied Mueller, "is to endure great trials. I have learned my faith by standing firm amid severe testing." Faith is learned, and we say this carefully, like any other skill — by practice. Just as a boxer must train for his struggle in the ring, so the individual Christian, if he wishes to be victorious, must practice faith as an everyday task. And just as the boxer purposely pits himself against a strong opponent in order to build up his physical and mental capacities, so the Christian must expect from God obstacles and afflictions, seemingly too great to bear, that his spiritual capacities might be increased.

MARCH
28
They feared the Lord, and served their own gods.
—II Kings 17:33

Men today, as they did back in King Hezekiah's time, still fear one God, and *serve* another. What does it mean to "fear God"? In our Scripture passage, the fear is merely a counterfeit, it does not ring true. It is only a superficial showing of outward respect, like the little boy who, after repeatedly being made to sit in a corner, finally told his mother, "I may be sitting down on the outside, but I'm still standing up inside!" The real fear of God is not lip worship but heart homage, an attitude of spirit in which the inner soul of a man is continually on its knees before God.

MARCH
29
He shall glorify Me.
—John 16:14

During the brilliant Victorian days in England, when those two great preachers were at their zenith — Parker at the City Temple and Spurgeon at the Metropolitan Tabernacle, the fashion for visitors in London was to hear Parker on Sunday morning and Spurgeon at night. An American visitor followed this procedure. His morning comment was, "My! what wonderful oratory!" His evening comment was, "Oh, what a wonderful Saviour!" Dear Spurgeon! — with him it was Jesus, *Jesus*, JESUS, all the time. And that is *always* the distinguishing trait when the Holy Spirit is filling a person or a ministry. The saintly old Dr. F. B. Meyer used to say, "In all real believers Jesus is *present*. In some He is not only present, but *prominent*. In others (all to few) He is not only present and prominent, He is pre-eminent." I wonder which of those three categories you and I belong to — present? or prominent? or pre-eminent? — J. SIDLOW BAXTER

Let this same attitude and purpose and [humble] mind be in you which was in Christ Jesus. — Let Him be your example in humility.
—Philippians 2:5 Amplified

Robert Murray M'Cheyne once said, "It is not great talents God blesses so much as great likeness to Jesus." In this day when many people judge a person's spiritual height by his "platform," or public, abilities, it is good for us to remember that our Lord and Saviour was basically a humble Man, even though, in the eyes of the world of His day, He became the greatest and most sought-after Teacher. Still, the Lord did not come into the world as royalty, but rather, He humbled Himself to the manger birth and a carpenter shop. If we are to follow His example, we will not seek service where we will be looked up to by men, but we will desire with all our hearts to be in the place where God wants us. Our primary purpose will be to mirror Jesus by the example of our lives.

About the fruit of the tree in the center of the garden God has said, You shall not eat of it or touch it, lest you die. —Genesis 3:3 Berkeley

Never put a question mark where God puts a period. Satan's strategy in tempting Eve was to plant a seed of doubt, to ask a question where God had made a flat statement of fact. Any temptation toward compromise or lowering of standards comes from the father of lies, Satan himself. Any temptation toward doubt comes from the planter of the seed of doubt, Satan himself. You as a child of God must, with open eyes and heart, unquestionably follow the leading of this God. The path of least resistance soon becomes a rut.

APRIL

APRIL 1

And as they were eating He said, Solemnly I say to you, one of you will betray Me!
—Matthew 26:21 Amplified

These are among the saddest words in the Bible. One becomes sadder still when he realizes that these same words could be truthfully spoken by Jesus to many so-called Christians today. Perhaps theirs is not such an obvious betrayal as that of Judas; nonetheless, they are as guilty of failing the Lord as was this infamous disciple. At times in our Christian lives all of us miss the mark. What a blessing it is to realize that genuine repentance and casting of ourselves anew on the mercy of God will bring forth His forgiveness. Even Judas might have been forgiven had he genuinely repented of his terrible deed.

APRIL 2

Pilate said to them, You have a guard of soldiers; [take them and] go, make it as secure as you can.
—Matthew 27:65 Amplified

What hint of future events must have led Pilate to leave this loophole, "as secure as you can"? With any ordinary man, no precautions need be taken to keep him within the grave. Life has departed — there is no danger of revival. But that is not the case with the Man, Christ Jesus! The sealing of the tomb was merely the beginning of His post-resurrection ministry, for He rose again in spite of all man could do to keep Him in the grave. We as Christian young people should rejoice in the tremendous power potential in our Lord and Saviour, Jesus Christ. Our Christian lives should be truly victorious when we realize that this same power potential is at our disposal.

APRIL 3

He is not here; He has risen, as He said [He would do]. Come, see the place where He lay.
—Matthew 28:6 Amplified

A good motto for the Christian life might well be, "Let me so live as though Jesus had died for me yesterday, rose this morning and is coming tomorrow." Truly, in the eyes of God, the momentous events of history are as closely woven as this. He sees the end from the beginning. All things are open to Him. If we really realized this, our lives would be different, for we would not try to hide anything from Him since we would be so completely aware of His all-seeing eye. If, on the other hand, we lived our lives in the awareness of His presence and precepts, how much more effective we would be! Let us remember that Jesus has done "as He said He would do!" And one of His promises was that He would be with us always!

APRIL 4

It is finished.
—John 19:30

Thank God, if as our Saviour said, "It is finished," for then there is nothing more to add. His Calvary work for salvation was all-sufficient and final. The Roman church's doctrine that we can add merit of our own to the Calvary work of Christ is a flagrant denial of plain Scripture teaching, and is an insult to the Saviour who cried, "It is finished." Somebody once asked a Christian believer, "How is it that you seem to have such peace, while I, although I go to church, do not have peace?" The Christian replied, "I think it is because yours is a religion of 'do,' while mine is a religion of 'done' — done once for all in my place by Jesus on Calvary." Real peace with God comes when we really believe on Christ in the sense of accepting His finished work of atonement for us.   — J. SIDLOW BAXTER

APRIL 5

And as thy servant was busy here and there, he was gone. —I Kings 20:40

A visitor in America once drove to Niagara Falls about which he had heard so much. He had come hundreds of miles to see the great sight. When about seven miles from the falls he thought he could hear the roar of water, and seeing a man in a field, he inquired, "Are those the falls I hear?" The man replied, "It could be, I don't know, but it could be. What of it if it is?" With surprise the visitor asked, "Do you live here?" "Born and raised here," was the answer. "And yet you don't know if that is the thunder of the falls?" "No, stranger," he said, "I have never seen them; I am too busy with my farm." Are you missing God's best today, because you are too busy?

— M. R. DeHaan

APRIL 6

And He said to them, [As for you] come away by yourselves to a deserted place, and rest a while. —Mark 6:31 Amplified

Christians today suffer from a common ailment — a shortage of time for meditation and spiritual communion with God. Just as it is impossible for a man to be physically healthy when he only takes two or three deep breaths of air a day, breathing shallowly the rest of the time, so it is impossible to be spiritually healthy on the strength of only a few moments of meaningful spiritual communion with God. The earthly man learns to breathe deeply as a habit and so the one who desires a deep spiritual life must make deep spiritual breathing a habit. True, it is not always possible to separate yourself from the world physically, but as Christians we can live in a spiritual atmosphere favorable to "waiting upon God."

APRIL 7

Know ye not, that to whom ye yield yourselves servants to obey, his servants ye are to whom ye obey; whether of sin unto death, or of obedience unto righteousness?
—Romans 6:16

Many have tried, but none have ever succeeded in serving both God and self. It simply does not work, for the devil soon monopolizes the part-time servant. Divided service misses out in both worlds. Saul, the tragic king of Israel, finally learned this. And Judas, infamous yet strikingly human, learned it and ended his life in desperation. On the other hand, those who succeeded in the Christian life could say with Paul, "This *one* thing I do." Mary "chose the better part," concentrating in the proper direction. Paul said pointedly, "For me to live is Christ." Only as we centralize our efforts and attentions in this way can we find true peace and satisfaction in the Christian life.

APRIL 8

Because thou art lukewarm, and neither cold nor hot, I will spue thee out of my mouth.
—Revelation 3:16

A number of years ago in Washington a man was returning from visiting friends one cold night in January when his train stopped suddenly. As it showed no disposition to move, he asked the conductor what was wrong. "A car is off the track ahead," he said. As cold as the night was, the man got off the train to investigate and found the car in such a position as to block progress entirely. He returned to the conductor and said: "It seems to me that the car is not off the track. If it were, we could go on." "That's right," said the trainman. "The trouble is it is partly on and partly off." So, too, those who hinder the work of Christ most are not so much the avowed unbelievers but rather nominal Christians who are "half on and half off the track."
— H. G. BOSCH

APRIL 9

Be a vessel set apart and useful for honorable and noble purposes, consecrated and profitable to the Master, fit and ready for any good work.
—II Timothy 2:21 Amplified

"Young men, do not pray for God to use you. . . ." Dr. J. Stewart Holden once said, pausing to allow the significance of his statement to sink into the consciousness of his listeners, then adding, "Pray that God will make you usable." Prayer should be logical, just as service should be logical. First things should come first, without question. If we are going to be of service to God, we should first be *fit* for service. And that requires the direct action of God Himself. The vessel must first be cleansed and emptied of all other contents, before it can be filled and used by God.

APRIL 10

My little children, I write you these things so that you may not violate God's law and sin; but if anyone should sin, we have an Advocate (One Who will intercede for us) with the Father. . . .
—I John 2:1 Amplified

"There are two ways of covering sin — man's way and God's way," D. L. Moody used to say. He then went on to point out that sins covered man's way are bound to have a resurrection, but sins covered *God's* way are placed where they never again can be uncovered. The Bible has four expressions to describe what God does with sins: "He casts them behind His back"; "He has blotted them out as a thick cloud"; "He casts them into the depths of the sea"; "He removes them as far as the East is from the West." We, as finite beings, cannot grasp the magnitude and thoroughness of God's removal of our sins. How God can forgive us, we cannot understand; all we *can* do, is to accept His Word and act upon it.

APRIL 11 *For me, to live is Christ — His life in me; and to die is gain — [the gain of the glory of eternity].*
—Philippians 1:21 Amplified

Spiritual riches are the only *true* riches. Spiritual friends are the only *real* friends. Temporal blessings are only temporary. If the central aim of our lives is to accumulate *things,* we will be of all men most miserable in eternity, for we will have made no preparation for life there. What is your main purpose in life? Can you say with Paul, "To die is gain"? Or will death separate you from your treasure?

APRIL 12 *Be still, and know that I am God. . . .*
—Psalm 46:10

Those who are able most efficiently to carry out their duties are those who can remain calm in the midst of the strains and distresses of modern-day living. Whether it be at work or at school, each of us needs the calm assurance of knowing God. And how can we know God? He has given us two avenues of approach to Him — the avenues of prayer and meditation upon His Word.

APRIL 13 *But without faith it is impossible to please and be satisfactory to God. For whoever would come near to God must (necessarily) believe that God exists and that He is the rewarder of those who earnestly and diligently seek Him (out).*
—Hebrews 11:6 Amplified

It was Martin Luther who often said to people who came to him with their problems, "Let God be God." To paraphrase his admonition, allow God to have His rightful place in your heart and life. You cannot say, "I and God" and expect God to lead you. It must be, "God and I." God first and myself second, God to lead and I to follow.

Is not this the carpenter's son?   —Matthew 13:55

All the wisdom of the world is mere child's play, yes, folly, compared with the knowledge of Christ. For what is more wonderful than to know and acknowledge the great, unspeakable mystery that the Son of God, the express Image of the Eternal Father, has taken our nature on Him and become in fashion as a man?

At Nazareth He must have helped His father build houses; for Joseph was a carpenter. Therefore Christ was called "the carpenter's son"; yes, Himself "the carpenter."

What will the people of Nazareth think at the Last Day, when they shall see Christ sitting in Divine Majesty, and may say to Him, "Lord, didst Thou not help build my house? How then camest Thou to this high glory?"

This, however, is the needful thing, that we Christians should with all diligence learn and know that the Son of God did so deeply humble Himself, was born so poor and in such a low estate, all on account of our sins; and that for our sakes He hid His Majesty so long.

— MARTIN LUTHER

Daniel gained insight in every kind of vision and dream.   —Daniel 1:17 Berkeley

"Insight" is certainly God-given and divinely inspired, in its final essence. That is why Christian young people, of all people, should excel in the intellectual realm. This was Daniel's secret of excellence, the will to learn which sustained him throughout his life and kept him in the forefront of his fellows, politically, physically and spiritually.

He only is my rock and my salvation. . . . He is my defense. . . .
—Psalm 62:2

Here are two symbols of what God is to His children. Anyone who has walked among the giant rocks of Colorado cannot help but be struck with the aptness of this symbol for strength. A rock may serve as a bulwark against an enemy before, as a shelter from an enemy above, and as a platform against an enemy below. In just the same sense, God is a bulwark, a shelter, and a platform or high place. But more than that, God is a defense, a "weapon," and we use the word carefully, to be taken into the battle both as a means of offense and defense. If you can use the Word of God, the Scriptures themselves, as a weapon, you will be a far more effective Christian than if you try to use weaker weapons!

The sheep that are My own hear and are listening to My voice, and I know them and they follow Me, And I give them eternal life. . . .
—John 10:27, 28 Amplified

How does one test His growth in the Lord? This verse gives the answer — by his ability to *hear* the Lord's voice. This, in essence, is spiritual discernment. Never before in the history of the world and the Church has spiritual discernment been more greatly needed! A further test of growth in grace is found in the next phrase, "And they follow Me." Discernment must be followed by obedience and each successive experience in following sharpens the spiritual ears of the disciple. Conversely, disobedience and refusal to follow tends to dull the spiritual ear. It is significant that the last phrase, "And I give them eternal life," follows in the wake of listening obedience. Oh, that every child of God might have a listening and obedient ear!

APRIL 18 *Then God said: Let us make man in Our likeness. . . . So God created man in His image.*
—Genesis 1:26, 27 Berkeley

"The Bible says" is almost the trademark of the world famous evangelist, Billy Graham. And how thankful God's children should be for the simple truth of this simple statement. Evolutionists would have us believe we have descended (or ascended) from a monkey, but the Bible tells us plainly that man was made in the image of God. Not only so, but God later declared, after He had seen everything that He had made, including man, that everything He had made was "excellent." No earthly builder would dare make this claim — only God is perfect. We should be thankful that our salvation, our very lives, rests on the foundation of One not subject to life's imperfections.

APRIL 19 *Abram dwelled in the land of Canaan and Lot dwelt in the cities of the plain and pitched his tent toward Sodom.* —Genesis 13:12

Take a look at Lot. In today's world Lot would have been known as "sharp" and shrewd in the business world. When he had a chance to choose, he chose what was apparently the best land, what was apparently the most enjoyable society. But he chose outside of the will of God, whereas Abraham chose to remain in God's will, accepting what was outwardly "second best." Lot put material riches first, and his material riches failed him completely. Ultimately he lost everything of earthly gain. Abraham, on the other hand, put God first, and received from God's hand a multitude of material blessings. Lot's way is the way of the world, the way which ends in emptiness. Abraham chose the better part and was rewarded throughout eternity for his faithfulness to God. Learn from His tragic experience.

APRIL 20

Just think of Him Who endured from sinners such grievous opposition and bitter hostility against Himself. . . . —Hebrews 12:3 Amplified

My prayer for all of us is that we will be willing to give up our good things in order to receive God's best.

Listen! God has wonder-filled plans for each one of us. We need to seek Him, look to Him and listen, so that we will learn what God is chiseling and grinding us for. Each one of our lives is like a block of marble. We can simply remain an unshapely lump, or we can watch the chips and dust fill the air as God makes something beautiful out of that rough piece of marble.

My heart aches for the people today who are running aimlessly here and there "killing time" because they have not thought of Him whose death on the Cross effectively killed time once and for all and opened wide the gates to heaven. Come! Enter in. Think of Him. — BETTY CARLSON

APRIL 21

It is better, (more profitable and wholesome) for you to enter life with only one eye than with two eyes to be thrown into the hell (Gehenna) of fire. —Matthew 18:9 Amplified

Which is the most serious — a physical disability or a spiritual handicap? According to our Lord, those who are physically disabled but spiritually whole or complete are more fortunate than those who are physically whole but spiritually imperfect. In short, as a young person, be more concerned about your spiritual condition than your physical condition. Be more greatly perturbed about spiritual imperfection than about physical lacks or disabilities. This does not mean that one should be unappreciative of his physical health, for such is certainly a great gift of God. But one should be even more thankful for the spiritual.

APRIL 22

From the ground the Lord God caused every tree to sprout that is pleasing to the eye and good for food. —Genesis 2:9 Berkeley

God could have created fruit that was "square" and black, trees with dingy leaves — but He didn't. Rather, He combined beauty with usefulness, loveliness with nutrition. Just so, He can take a life that is dark and useless and make of it something beautiful and blessedly useful.

APRIL 23

To make it your ambition and definitely endeavor to live quietly and peacefully, to mind your own affairs and to work with your hands. . . . —I Thessalonians 4:11 Amplified

God has given each of His children a job to do, a duty to perform. As each one of us carries out his own personal responsibility, God's will and work is carried out. Whenever one of His children fails in his responsibility, the chain of God's purpose is weakened proportionately.

APRIL 24

. . . Lest I cause my brother to be tripped up and fall and to offend. —I Corinthians 8:13 Amplified

"Am I my brother's keeper?" is an age-old question, flung into the face of God by Cain, one of the first men to rebel against divine judgment. It is a question we must face today in all areas of life — our Christian conduct, our spiritual concern, our example to those weaker than ourselves in the Christian life. If any action of ours, public or private, causes our weaker brother to stumble and fall, and we act unconcerned and irresponsible, we are answering Cain's question with a "No." But if we take as our standard for life the word and example of our Saviour, we must answer "Yes" to Cain's question and look to God for the strength to carry out our commitment.

APRIL 25

Whosoever shall do the will of God, the same is my brother and my sister, and mother.

—Mark 3:35

This seems too good to be true. To be the brother or the sister of Jesus — did you ever try to think out what it means? Then for every Christian to be taken by Christ into as close and tender a relationship as His own mother sustained to Him — did you ever try to think that out, remembering that you are the one taken into this loving fellowship?

But we must not overlook the first part of this verse, that tells us *who* are received into this close relationship — "whosoever shall do the will of God." At every point as we go on, we catch more and more distinctly the teaching that obedience to God is part of the faith that saves. We must do God's will, and follow Christ wholeheartedly if we would obtain the privilege of being the brothers and sisters of Christ.

— J. R. MILLER

APRIL 26

And when the ark of the covenant of the Lord came into the camp, all Israel shouted. . . .

—I Samuel 4:5

The Israelites here were making a greater fuss about the ark than they were about the Lord. Their religion had regressed to the point of substitution. When the *object* of worship becomes secondary to the *means* of worship, substitution has arrived. The popular concept of prayer as a magic cure-all is a case in point. True prayer is fellowship with God, not a pleading with God to answer one's demands. Another case in point is the popularity of the cross as an ornament, when actually the cross is a symbol of terrible crucifixion. We should worship the Christ of the cross. Let us "shout" about the Lord, not about the ark!

APRIL
27
Neither give place to the devil. —Ephesians 4:27

A teacher in a Bible school gave his students two subjects for their examination paper. They were to write a half hour on each of the two subjects, the Holy Spirit and the devil. One student wrote steadily for an hour on the first subject, the Holy Spirit, and then wrote a note at the bottom of his manuscript, "I had no time for the devil." He had been so busy with the Holy Spirit that he had no place for the devil. This is the only way in which we can resist and overcome Satan. The Holy Spirit has left us the Word of God. If we fill ourselves with God's Word and prayer and witness for Christ, then we shall not "give place to the devil." — M. R. DeHaan

APRIL
28
Come now, and let us reason together, saith the Lord: Though your sins be as scarlet, they shall be as white as snow; though they be red like crimson, they shall be as wool. —Isaiah 1:18

The trade mark of many religious exhorters today seems to be, "Ours not to reason why, ours is to do or die." In other words, the individual Christian does not need to understand or be logical about his position in Christ or how he arrived there. This is contrary to the Word of God, however; for God says, according to Isaiah, that the Christian life is a *reasonable* one, one arrived at by logical steps. This does not preclude the possibility of a young child's coming into a saving knowledge of Christ. In fact, the simplicity of the plan of salvation is often the very stumbling block in the path of the sophisticated, while the child's uncomplicated acceptance of God at His Word makes it possible for him to accept the divine presentation. Yes, we Christian young people can certainly give a "reason for the hope that is within us"!

APRIL
29
And she (Hagar) called the name of the Lord that spake unto her, Thou God seest me. . . .
—Genesis 16:13

Hagar was fleeing from an uncomfortable and disagreeable situation. Abraham's wife, Sarah, jealous of Hagar, had virtually told Abraham, "It is either Hagar or I — take your choice!" But Hagar could not flee from the sight of God nor His care for her. In fact, in her flight she learned submission to the will of God. She returned to Abraham's tent where she remained with her son, Ishmael, until after Isaac's birth. No, fleeing a disagreeable situation does not help. The Lord Jesus did not flee Gethsemane or the cross — even though He knew what torture and terrible death awaited Him. Rest in the promise of "Thou God seest me," realizing that no matter what befalls you, your Heavenly Father sees and cares.

APRIL
30
And again Peter denied (knowing Christ).
—John 18:27 Amplified

Could this be the same disciple who had been surnamed "the rock" by the Lord Himself? Could this be the same Peter who, unafraid, preached to the scribes and pharisees on Pentecost? The Lord Jesus must have looked deep into the heart of Peter, beyond the weak human shell which would yield and break, down to the rock-like core of courage which would eventually stand the test. How encouraging it is to think upon Peter when we ourselves become discouraged with our own weakness and failure, for in Peter we have an object lesson of what the Lord can do with even the weakest of men. Once a little maid could make Peter tremble — but on the anvil of God, Peter's character was formed until he could courageously die a martyr's death, unafraid and completely victorious in Christ.

MAY

MAY 1

And if Christ be not raised, your faith is vain; ye are yet in your sins. . . . But now is Christ risen from the dead. —I Corinthians 15:17, 20

Many of us think a great deal about John and Peter, Augustine and Calvin, Wesley and Whitefield; we know much about them. But we cannot contact them or know them personally, for they are long since buried and departed. Nor can any Buddhist or Mohammedan know Buddha or Mohammed by direct contact today. Nay, the very suggestion would be ridiculed as absurd by their devotees; for like all other mortals, Buddha and Mohammed succumbed to death, and their spirits fled from this earthly scene centuries ago. How then could Paul, in Philippians 3:10, claim to know Jesus personally and continually? How can we ourselves claim to know Him? It is because HE IS ALIVE. — J. SIDLOW BAXTER

MAY 2

The kingdom of heaven is like something precious buried in a field, which a man found . . . then in his joy he goes and sells all he has and buys that field. . . . like a man who is . . . in search of finding precious pearls, who, on finding a single pearl of great price went and sold all he had and bought it. —Matthew 13:44-46 Amplified

The man and the merchant in Jesus' parable had one thing in common — a willingness to give everything they had in return for what was most precious to them. That is the way a Christian young person should feel about the precious possession of salvation which is his. Consecrate everything you have and are in appreciation for this gift.

MAY 3 *And whoever [earnestly] desires to do it, let him come and take and appropriate (drink) the Water of Life without cost.* —Revelation 22:17 Amplified

Permanent quenching of physical thirst is impossible. But, permanent quenching of spiritual thirst is blessedly possible at the fountain of Life itself, the Lord Jesus Christ. It is necessary however, to *stoop* down to drink — in the physical as well as the spiritual sense. This water is truly without cost — but it demands humility and surrender. So, as did the Samaritan woman at the well, first receive this water of life freely for yourself, then go out and tell the Good News to others!

MAY 4 *He inevitably deludes himself who attempts to delude God. For whatever a man sows, that and that only is what he will reap.* —Galatians 6:7 —Amplified

Youth is traditionally the time for the sowing of "wild oats." In some cases this exuberance of youth results in little more than harmless pranks. Unfortunately, however, in today's world altogether too many young people are traveling, unrestrained, down the broad road to destruction, mistakenly thinking they are only sowing a few harmless "wild oats." The Christian life is definitely not to be unhappy and "sour," but the Christian life must be realistic. If we face life realistically, we realize with Paul, that "what goes up must come down." We reap what we sow! How much better then to follow the wisdom of Solomon who said, "To him that soweth righteousness shall be a sure reward" (Proverbs 11:18). A little realistic thinking now will save vain regret in the future.

MAY 5

But when the young man heard this, he went away sad (grieved and in much distress), for he had great possessions. —Matthew 19:22 Amplified

Dr. F. B. Meyer has told us how his early Christian life was marred and his ministry paralyzed just because he had kept back one key from the bunch of keys to his heart which he had given the Lord. Every key save one! The key of one room of his heart was kept for personal use, and the Lord was shut out. And the effects of this incomplete consecration were found in lack of power, lack of assurance, lack of joy and peace. The "joy of the Lord" begins when we hand over the last key. We sit with Christ on His throne as soon as we have surrendered all our crowns, and made Him sole and only ruler of our life and its possessions.

— J. H. JOWETT

MAY 6

. . . as a hen gathereth her chickens under her wings. —Matthew 23:37

Whoever invented the word "chicken-hearted" didn't know his chickens. "Chicken-hearted," according to Webster, means to be timid, afraid, fearful, or cowardly. In modern teen-age jargon, anyone without courage is "chicken." I spring to the defense of the grossly maligned fowl, for a chicken is just the opposite. I have never seen a greater demonstration of courage, fearlessness, and loyalty than I have seen displayed by a chicken in the time of danger. A hen will sit immovable through the most violent gale, her chicks gathered safely beneath her, that they might be protected from the storm without. Perhaps now we can understand better why Jesus compared His own love to that of a hen who "doth gather her brood under her wings" (Luke 13:34). — M. R. DeHaan

MAY 7   *And they (His fellow countrymen) took offense at Him. . . .* —Matthew 13:57 Amplified

Here is a good verse for those of you who have become discouraged in trying to deal with your loved ones on eternal matters. Jesus apparently did not become discouraged when His own townspeople failed to be moved by His teachings and convinced by His claims. Neither should we as Christians become discouraged when our witness apparently falls on stony ground, when our parents and loved ones seem cold and hard. My responsibility, after all, is merely to sow the seed — the Holy Spirit is the One who must bring it to fruition. Discouragement deadens the effectiveness of the Christian's witness; that is why I must be willing to rest in God's divine plan and care.

MAY 8   *You have heard of the endurance of Job; and you have seen the Lord's [purpose and how He richly blessed him in the] end, in as much as the Lord is full of pity* and *compassion* and *tenderness and mercy.* —James 5:11 Amplified

It is not always easy to endure, to wait, particularly if we are called upon to endure testing such as Job endured. It is often difficult to see the hand of the Lord in rough circumstances. But if we remember as Jeremiah did in Lamentations 3, that "His compassions fail not: they are new every morning," then we can look beyond our immediate circumstances toward our ultimate destination, eternal fellowship with God. Just as God works through the cold and snow of winter to prepare the ground for planting and harvest, He often works through adversity and difficulty to prepare our hearts for eternity.

MAY 9

For he reasoned that God was able to raise [him] up even from among the dead.
—Hebrews 11:19 Amplified

It has been said, "One plus God is a majority." Abraham certainly lived out his belief in this equation. This is the type of faith that leads one into great adventure with God. It is not we who accomplish, however; it is God. Our God is unbeatable and unbeaten.

MAY 10

For in him, we live, and move, and have our being. . . .
—Acts 17:28

God the Lord gives daily water from the rocks; bread from the sand; vegetables of all kinds from the earth. But because He gives these lavishly, without ceasing, no man holds it to be a miracle. The blind world, forgetting Him, thinks that all comes by chance. But, on the other hand, those who love Him, whithersoever they turn their eyes, whether to the heavens or the earth, the air or the water, they see pure, obvious miracles of God. — MARTIN LUTHER

MAY 11

If we confess our sins, he is faithful and just to forgive us our sins.
—I John 1:9

Someone has said, "Unconfessed sin in the soul is like a bullet in the body." Such a wound cannot be ignored. If left untreated, it will eventually cause death, just as certainly as the bite of a poisonous snake. Allowing unconfessed sin to remain in one's life will lead to spiritual death. This concept does not nullify the sacrifice of Christ on Calvary. It is as if an antidote for poison were left unused on the shelf. Unless God's forgiveness is sincerely sought, an unconfessed sin may become the barrier between you and eternal life.

MAY 12

Save me, I pray, from my brother's hand . . . for I fear him, that he may come and slay me. . . .
—Genesis 32:11 Berkeley

Jacob was well advised to fear his powerful brother, Esau — especially in view of his treacherous treatment of Esau when the brothers were only teen-agers. "Be sure your sins will find you out" is a warning too often ignored by young people. The best insurance against having your "chickens come home to roost" is to live righteously.

MAY 13

I will never leave thee, nor forsake thee.
—Hebrews 13:5

There was a Hebrew prophet once who thought to sail beyond the reach of "the presence of the Lord." Had he only read certain verses from the Pentateuch for his Scripture reading that morning, or a few verses from Psalm 139, he would never have paid his fare. Later, he was grateful to find that even his strange submarine inside the "great fish" could not shut him off from God. What a comfort the presence of the Lord was to Paul as he took his trial before Nero! — "At my first defence no man stood with me, but all men forsook me: I pray God that it may not be laid to their charge. Notwithstanding, the Lord stood with me, and strengthened me." And how real has the Lord's presence been to multitudes of others! One could fill books with testimonies. The danger is that in picking out examples we should give the impression that such realization of His presence is only for a favorite few. No, God is not a respecter of persons. The supporting consciousness of His presence may be known by the humblest among us.
— J. SIDLOW BAXTER

MAY 14

So they answered Jesus, We do not know. And He said to them, Nor will I tell you by what power of authority I do these things.
—Matthew 21:27 Amplified

In this instance, Jesus was speaking to the unbelieving chief priests and elders. But sometimes He denies even His own children an answer when they question. After all, isn't it His prerogative as Creator to keep His own counsel? Doesn't He have a right to expect from us unquestioning obedience? If we would learn this lesson, our Christian experience would lose its "up and down" motion.

MAY 15

He (Jesus) said to them (the disciples), Why are you so timid and fearful? How is it that you have no faith — no firmly relying trust?
—Mark 4:40 Amplified

Almost two thousand years have passed, and though we know more in some ways than these men to whom Jesus spoke, yet in time of strain and stress we are still driven to say, "Who then is this?" In the answer to that question lies the secret of rest and deliverance from fear. In the degree that we know Him, in that degree shall we be fearless and quiet amid all the commotions of life.   —UNGER

MAY 16

Put on the whole armour of God . . . to stand against . . . the devil.
—Ephesians 6:10

You have to be willing to do more than just "stand" to effectively withstand the wiles of the evil one. Men with trained intellect combined with godly determination are needed in this never-ending battle, the stakes of which are life itself! Where is one to find the needed armor to stand against the subtlety of the evil one? Only in consecrated surrender to the Spirit of God.

MAY 17

God said: Let there be lights in the firmament . . .
to shed light upon the earth; and it was so.
—Genesis 1:14, 15 Berkeley

Living the Christian life is a *personal* matter and responsibility. Each Christian, in his own way, is responsible to shed his share of God's light. This does not mean that God's light comes from inside the individual Christian — but God's light *is reflected* by individual Christians. Each one brings out some aspects of the Light which is peculiarly his own. It is the blending of the individual lights which results in the impact of the one great Light. This is the reason why it is so important for each of us as Christians to be faithful and consistent in lighting the world.

MAY 18

Work out — cultivate, carry out to the goal and fully complete — your own salvation with reverence and awe and trembling [self-distrust, that is, with serious caution, tenderness of conscience, watchfulness against temptation; timidly shrinking from whatever might offend God and discredit the name of Christ.] —Philppians 2:12 Amplified

It has been said that one's reputation is what the world sees, but one's character is what he is in the dark. That must have been the distinction that Paul had in mind as he wrote these words to the Philippians. We do not work out our own salvation in the sense that we earn this eternal gift. No, it is purely and simply a gift from God. However, in many cases the only Bible ever read by the world is the life of the Christian. If God's Word "works out" through that life, then we are "living epistles." On the other hand, if our lives do not reveal God, then, in effect, we have closed God's book to those who need its message. In that sense, we must "work out" our salvation.

The Lord gave the word . . . .   —Psalm 68:11

The Bible is not a thing to be worshiped. A savage might bow down to a telescope, but an astronomer knows better. The way to know a telescope is to use it. It is not to be looked at, but to look through. To bind a Bible beautifully, to lift it reverently, to speak of it with admiration, to guard it with all care, is not at all to the point. Look through it. Find God with it. See what God was to the men of the Bible, and then let Him be the same to you. See the proofs of His power, and prove that power for yourself, in yourself. Search the Scriptures for the testimony of Jesus, and honor the Scriptures by being an honor to the One they reveal.   — M. D. BABCOCK

. . . I am the Lord, and I will bring you out from under the burdens. . . .   —Exodus 6:6

If some were to make this promise, we could take it "with a grain of salt," as it were. But notice that God prefaces this promise with the statement, "I am the Lord." That is all the qualification He needs to give to convince us of His ability. Wherever we look in the Word of God we are impressed with the "all-powerfulness" of this our God. So, we can take Him at His Word, and proceed without fear on the basis of His promise. If we have burdens, He has promised to bring us out from under them. In other words, He will take over the burden and leave us with the blessing. Perhaps others could take over our burden for a while, but eventually we would find it back upon our shoulders. Not so with God. He is the only One with "what it takes" to assume our burdens permanently and conclusively.

**MAY
21**
*Finally, all [of you] should be of one and the
same mind (united in spirit), sympathizing [with
one another], loving [each the others] as brethren
(of one household). . . .* —I Peter 3:8 Amplified

Peter speaks here of something more than mere unison
— this is harmony. The essence of harmony can best be
illustrated by the marvelous result of the "working together" of the large modern symphony orchestra. If all of
the instruments merely played in unison, how "lifeless" their
contribution would be. But when each member plays his
own instrument, with a variety of scores combining to
make rich and beautiful harmony, that's something different!
The same is true of a field of wild flowers — the greater
the variety of color, the more perfect the result to the eyes.
This is the way it should be among Christians, each one
performing his God-given task in harmony with his fellows —
harmony built on common faith in an uncommon Lord.

**MAY
22**
*Your forefather Abraham was extremely happy at
the hope and prospect of seeing My day [My
incarnation]. And he did see it and was delighted.*
—John 8:56 Amplified

Abraham had a marvelous spiritual vision. He saw
more than 1800 years into the future — without the aid
of astronomical instruments — before he died! I wonder
about my spiritual vision. Is my contact with God close
enough and vital enough — or am I dwelling "afar off"?
Genesis 25:8 says of Abraham, ". . . at a ripe old age, after
a long and full life, Abraham expired" (Berkeley). That
epitaph should be written over the life of every Christian.
The length of life is not the important thing — it is the
quality of it that counts! And quality comes from a right
relationship to God.

MAY 23

There is no fear in love — dread does not exist; (full-grown, complete, perfect) love turns fear out of doors and expels every trace of terror!
—I John 4:18 Amplified

Fear of the future is a common plague, at the root of most suicides and mental breakdowns. But for the Christian, this life is merely a pilgrimage, a journey from one point to another. At the close of this life, people who have not trusted their future to Christ see nothing ahead but a grave and an uncertain destination beyond it; the Christian, on the other hand, can look forward to a future bright with the constant presence of the risen Saviour. Thus, the Christian may live today to the full, completely rid of the fear that plagues most men in these days.

MAY 24

I want you to say you are my sister, so that I may be favored on your account, and because of you my life will be spared. —Genesis 12:13 Berkeley

The same Abraham who had obeyed God without question and in faith, now resorts to falsehood and deceit to protect his life — instead of trusting the Lord who had led him so faithfully. Thus, even the most godly of men are tempted aside from the path of perfect obedience by too much concern for self. In spite of Abraham's spiritual negligence, however, God remained faithful and brought him out of the difficulty into which his lies had led him. Even so today, our God remains faithful in the midst of our unfaithfulness. It is sobering to think that even our little exaggerations and our "white lies" come between us and our Saviour. We must allow Him to remove these shortcomings from our lives.

MAY 25

Then I said, I have laboured in vain, I have spent my strength for naught, and in vain.

—Isaiah 49:4

Mind, it is our best work that He wants, not the dregs of our exhaustion. I think He must prefer quality to quantity. — GEORGE MACDONALD

If the people about you are carrying on their business or their benevolence at a pace which drains the life out of you, resolutely take a slower pace; be called a laggard, make less money, accomplish less work than they, but be what you were meant to be and can be. You have your natural limit of power as much as an engine, ten-horse power, or twenty, or a hundred. You are fit to do certain kinds of work, and you need a certain kind and amount of fuel, and a certain kind of handling. — GEORGE S. MERRIAM

In your occupations, try to possess your soul in peace. It is not a good plan to be in haste to perform any action that it may be the sooner over. On the contrary, you should accustom yourself to do whatever you have to do with tranquility, in order that you may retain the possession of yourself and of settled peace. — MADAME GUYON

MAY 26

God made the two great luminaries, the greater light for ruling the day and the lesser light with the stars for ruling the night.

—Genesis 1:16 Berkeley

Why all the rush to reach the moon in this modern space age? In God's eyes, the moon is a lesser luminary, yet men are more concerned with reaching this "created" planet than they are of coming into touch with the greater light, the Son of Light, the Creator Himself. It is so typical of human understanding to put lesser things first, to ignore things of primary importance.

MAY 27   *God said, . . . Let birds fly. . . . God also created the large sea-monsters. . . .*
—Genesis 1:20, 21 Berkeley

How great is God! His Word made not only the giant whale but also the tiny, delicate humming bird. Should you hesitate to entrust your life to such a One as this? The One with whom we have to do is far greater than our limited concept of Him — and He is far more capable of keeping His children than the most loving earthly parent.

MAY 28   *For Herod had arrested John and . . . put him in prison. . . .*   —Matthew 14:3 Amplified

One wonders why Jesus did not use His God-given power to release John the Baptist from prison. Instead, He sent John's disciples back to the prisoner with encouraging words about His own ministry, words which must have strengthened the Baptist's faith even in his last moments before his death at the hands of Herod. It is often difficult for us, with our finite understanding, to understand the workings of an infinite God. John's death must have thrown his disciples into confusion, but it was the means God used to lead them into a saving knowledge of the Lord.

MAY 29   *For out of His fullness (abundance) we all received.*
—John 1:16 Amplified

God does not show favoritism among His children. There is no God-given grace provided to one of your fellow-Christians that is not available to you as well. Has it been your impression that God could not bring forth another Luther, Calvin, Spurgeon, or Graham in this day? God has already done His part — it only remains for some young person to say with Moody, "By God's grace, I will be that man."

MAY 30

For truly, I say to you, if you have faith [that is living] like a grain of mustard seed, you can say to this mountain, Move from here to yonder place, and it will move and nothing will be impossible to you. —Matthew 17:20 Amplified

Just as Jesus' disciples seem to have been "playing around" as far as their depth of faith was concerned, you and I are often likewise guilty of "playing in the sand pile" when we should be "moving the mountain." We often hear of tremendous victories in the lives of other Christians, but we forget that there has been genuine work involved in achieving that victory. Jesus warned His disciples ". . . this kind does not go out except by prayer and fasting." The kind of faith that moves mountains is a serious, realistic relationship to the God from whom this faith comes. Subject your faith to close examination to see if it measures up.

MAY 31

Thou, O Lord, art a shield for me; my glory and the lifter up of mine head. —Psalm 3:3

This short psalm is the song of a sorrowful soul who found help and comfort in the Lord. David says, "How are they increased that trouble me." But then he thanks the Lord for being a shield between him and his tormentors. God is the only One sufficiently strong to "stand off" the adverse circumstances of life. David then adds, "My glory," the glory which cannot be touched by the dirt of the world, the glory which cannot be dimmed by the actions of the godless. With such a God, and such a glory, how can the child of God be anything but "lifted up"? "I will lift up mine eyes toward the hills, from whence cometh my help," says David in another psalm, fully realizing that even in such a simple act as "looking upward" God has the decisive part.

JUNE

JUNE 1 . . . *Christ within* and *among you the hope of [realizing] the glory.* —Colossians 1:27 Amplified

The story is told of one who underwent operation after operation for the removal of a small piece of broken needle which had lodged in his eye. Each operation had driven that little irritating object deeper into the sensitive organ until he was in danger of losing his sight. Finally a young doctor thought of a new way to handle the case. Leaving his probes and other delicate instruments in his bag, he used a small but powerful magnet, holding it as close to the eye as he dared. Immediately the small piece of steel needle began to move outward toward the magnet, soon leaving the wounded eye and relieving the sufferer. This method was as simple as it was successful. By a single touch, the eye was saved and the trouble overcome. In just the same way, the power and attraction of Christ works in the life of the sinner, removing the irritation of the old life and providing power to live the new life.

JUNE 2 *But I say, walk and live habitually in the (Holy) Spirit.* . . . —Galatians 5:16 Amplified

If you have ever been in love or have known two people in love, you know what Paul means in this verse when he says, "If you are so 'wrapped up' in the Holy Spirit, you will not even see the things of the world going on around you." Two people in love have eyes only for each other. They can be in the center of a hube crowd and see only each other. Their surroundings mean nothing to them. It is as if the surroundings were not even there. That is the way it can be with a Christian if he is truly "in love" with the One who loved him so supremely. If you are bothered by the things of the world, in the sense that they tempt you to the point of surrender, you will find victory only in an even greater surrender to the God of your salvation.

JUNE 3 *But these are written, that ye might believe that Jesus is the Christ, the Son of God; and that believing ye might have life through his name.*
—John 20:31

The gospel of John was written in order that we might believe that Jesus is the Christ. The First Epistle of John was written to people who believe that Jesus is the Christ but who have never come into full assurance of their present position or of the possession of eternal life. "These things have I written unto you that believe on the name of the Son of God; that ye may know that ye have eternal life, and that ye may believe on the name of the Son of God" (I John 5:13). If you have any doubt concerning the atoning death of Christ or about His deity, read the Gospel of John; but if you have believed the message of the Gospel and you are still perplexed as to the question of assurance, read the Epistle of John. Everywhere I go people come to me and ask me how they may *know*. . . .

There are thousands of young people who think they are saved, but in reality, when they take the acid test, they find they have never been born again of the Spirit of God. If they died they would never go to heaven. So let us take the test. Let us examine ourselves. Let us check and see how we stand in the light of God's Word. . . .

— BILLY GRAHAM

JUNE 4   *Now then, you do whatever God has told you.*
                                          —Genesis 31:16 Berkeley

How blessed is the man whose wife says to him, "Do whatever God has told you," as was the case with Jacob here. Every Christian young person should be concerned that the one with whom he takes the marriage vow is one who is wholly committed to God's will. There is no alliance so troubling and discouraging as that of the consecrated Christian with the carnal unbeliever — yet, all too often, in this day of rapid courtships and hasty marriages, young people find themselves regretting at leisure a marriage they have formed in haste. This all-important step should never be taken thoughtlessly or hastily. Rather, the choice of a life's companion should be subjected to the scrutiny of God's Word and will, not an action taken hastily.

JUNE 5   *Freely (without pay) you have received; freely (without charge) give.* —Matthew 10:8 Amplified

As Christians, we are commanded and challenged to give *ourselves.* And this must be a continuing process, just as our growth in Christ is a continuing and constant forward movement. While still at Wheaton College, Jim Elliot wrote, "One does not surrender a life in an instant. That which is lifelong can only be surrendered in a lifetime."° What a depth of spiritual wisdom for one who had just attained legal voting age. Many Christians *never* learn this lesson. As my life grows spiritually, my surrender of it to Christ must grow deeper and greater. And as I grow spiritually, my surrendered life becomes that much more valuable in God's program for His Church.

° From *Shadow of the Almighty* by Elisabeth Elliot. Used by permission of the publishers, Harper and Brothers, New York.

JUNE 6 *Godliness accompanied with contentment—that con is great and abundant gain.* —I Timothy 6:6
—Amplified

Contentment, or satisfaction, is not found in outward circumstances or situations — and contentment alone is not enough. No, contentment comes from an inner stock of strength, and that stock is drawn from godliness, a close walk with the Creator and Sustainer of life. Paul tells young Timothy here that true riches are the riches of the spirit, rather than material gain, and logically, as only he can present logic, Paul points out to Timothy that since worldly goods remain in the world and cannot be transported, material things then are not a source of true happiness and contentment. The only lasting sufficiency is that inward peace of a right relationship to God through His Son, the Lord Jesus — spiritual riches.

JUNE 7 *God is love, and he who dwells and continues in love dwells and continues in God, and God dwells and continues in him.* —I John 4:16
—Amplified

The essence of true love can only be found in God Himself. "God commended his love toward us, in that, while we were yet sinners, Christ died for us." God's example in love, then, is one of sacrifice — a sacrifice keeps on, *continues* giving, as John here points out. In the same way, the Christian life should be one of *continuing* love. Tolstoy said, "When you love a person, you do for that person what that person needs." That definition of love in action may certainly be applied to Christ's sacrifice on Calvary. If it is also characteristic of our love both toward God and toward our fellow men, then how noticeable, how *real* our love will be!

JUNE 8

The life I now live in the body I live by faith — by adherence to and reliance on and [complete] trust — in the Son of God. . . .
— Galatians 2:20 Amplified

The Christian life was never meant to run on the battery system. It was meant to run on the *electric circuit principle.* You know what that is. Put simply, it is just this: continuous *current* through continuous *contact.* You and I have no power over the current; but we do have power over the contact; and when, by regular prayer-times, daily meditation in the written Word, consecration to Christ, and separation from unworthy ways, we maintain the "contact," then the heavenly current, the Holy Spirit, the life of Christ, is continuously communicated to us.

— J. SIDLOW BAXTER

JUNE 9

In this is love, not that we love God, but that He loved us and sent His Son to be the propitiation (the atoning sacrifice) for our sins.
— I John 4:10 Amplified

John goes on to say, "Beloved, if God loved us so [very much], we also ought to love one another" (vs. 11). Our purpose in keeping the commandments of God should not be based on the thought of reward or commandment, but on the sublime foundation of love. The world today is so filled with hatred and violence that the faintest breath of love seems like a spring in the desert. Yet, if every Christian lived a life whose foundation and purpose was to show God's love to others, the desert of this world would blossom as the rose! An attitude of love is contrary to the natural man outside of Christ — but should be a "built-in" characteristic of the Christian's daily walk.

JUNE 10

Upon hearing his father's words, Esau wailed with a most loud and bitter cry, pleading with his father, "Bless me, too, my father."

Genesis 27:34 Berkeley

Little things often determine destiny. Hasty decisions are often regretted in the end. All because he yielded to his overwhelming physical hunger, Esau missed the great spiritual blessing God had reserved and labeled for Isaac's descendants. Just as unthinkingly, you and I may make the wrong decision and miss God's best for us.

JUNE 11

This is My commandment, that you love one another [just] as I have loved you. —John 15:12

—Amplified

Only recently have I had any appreciation of what it cost God to love me, and I am beginning to see people in a totally different light. It is not a bright light. There is a softness about the light beneath the Cross. Photographers know how important shadows and angles are. When I compare my passport picture with the touched up one my mother has on her dresser, it's like looking at two different people. Yes, shadows and angles do a lot to soften people. When we look at people in the light of the Cross, we find it casts a shadow across the faults of others, their weaknesses, their stupidities, their dullness, their petty ways — and most mercifully, we find God's love and forgiveness broad enough to cover all of our transgressions and shortcomings as well as theirs.

Not only do we change, but also the people around us change when we start loving them in this revolutionary way. If you want to get along with people, you can. Try loving them. We can never be the same, once we start giving out the love of God. — BETTY CARLSON

JUNE 12

(Esau) ate and drank, then got up and went his way. So lightly did Esau esteem his birthright.
—Genesis 25:34 Berkeley

A healthy appetite is a great physical blessing, but physical desires should not interfere with spiritual growth. Esau forfeited spiritual blessing for the appeasement of a temporary physical hunger. In much the same way, carnal Christians allow fleshly desires to "clog up" the channel of spiritual blessing at the hand of God. Make your life motto, "Seek ye first the kingdom of God. . . ." But realize that if you put the fleshly first, you will miss the best in life, sacrificing spiritual blessing on the altar of immediate pleasure, forfeiting eternal dividends for current "spending money."

JUNE 13

And receiving an answer to their asking, they were divinely instructed and warned. . . .
—Matthew 2:12 Amplified

What is the key to wisdom? Where did these wise men gain their understanding? From the Lord Himself — after they asked! Where can you find the meaning of life? How do you discover the purpose of life? Not in books, though these often prove of supplementary value in a search for wisdom. Is study the answer? Not alone. For "the fear of the Lord is the beginning of wisdom." If you do not begin at the right point, you cannot hope to arrive at a satisfactory conclusion. "Without Me ye can do nothing," were the words of Jesus to His followers. If you begin with Him you are bound to reach your soul's destination, according to His promise and Word. Reap every benefit you can from the wisdom of the world, but begin with the wisdom that comes only from on high.

JUNE 14   *For all who are led by the Spirit of God are sons of God.*   —Romans 8:14 Amplified

What meaning is wrapped up in this brief verse! And at the same time, what a huge responsibility. Yes, if you know Christ as your Saviour, you are a "son" of God. But to reach this exalted position, you must surrender yourself to be "led" by the Spirit of God. You must come to the end of yourself in order to begin with God. Realize your own emptiness — then allow yourself to be filled with God's fullness. You need to realize your "lost" condition before you can be led out of the wilderness of your sins. Your only responsibility is repentance and recognition of your lost situation. God takes over from that point! And then you become a "son," with every privilege that offers.

JUNE 15   *These two commandments sum up and upon them depends all the Law and the prophets.*   —Matthew 22:40 Amplified

Someone has said, "The best way to spell law is L-O-V-E!" In fact, Jesus here sums up the five or six hundred Jewish laws in one colossal commandment—"Love the Lord and love your neighbors." It is significant that our love for those about us should be a reflection of our love for our God. There is no room here for petty jealousies or bickering. Rather, this command demands wholeheartedness and total commitment. And who are better equipped to fulfill this demand of God than young people, with their exuberant zeal and hearty enthusiasm? If Christian young people put into practice what the Lord here prescribes, what would be the effect upon the world around them? Just as love has a way of surmounting personal difficulties — it is equally effective in overcoming national and international tension.

JUNE
16
Children, obey your parents in the Lord.
—Ephesians 6:1 Amplified

How much is involved in this little word, "in"? Look at it this way: Would we ever see a rainbow if it were not revealed by the sunlight? Would we ever see the true beauty of autumn colors unless they were revealed by God's sunlight? It is as we see our parents as they are in the Lord, and obey them accordingly, that we begin to realize their true beauty. This is the secret of the Christian life as well. If we look upon everything that happens as being *"in* the Lord," we will be much happier in spite of what seems to be a difficult experience. *"In* Christ" lies the key that opens the door to all that is best. He is the Way. As we realize this, we will discover new richness in what might otherwise become the merely routine.

JUNE
17
Therefore put on God's complete armor, that you may be able to resist and stand your ground on the evil day [of danger], and having done all [the crisis demands], to stand [firmly in your place].
—Ephesians 6:13 Amplified

Thomas Carlyle once said, "You cannot fight the French merely with red uniforms. There must be men inside them!" Paul here gives us a description of a well-equipped soldier, able to stand against every foe. But the weapons of the soldier are on the inside! The Christian soldier is "strong in the Lord . . . empowered through . . . that strength which His [boundless] might provides" (Ephesians 6:10 Amplified). The Christian soldier draws his resources from God Himself. His weapons are truth, righteousness, plus faith and prayer — not a bomb or a cannon, which can fail. We should be thankful that our resources are in God not in man!

JUNE 18   *Then was Jesus led up of the spirit into the wilderness to be tempted of the devil.*   —Matthew 4:1

An old writer says: "All the while our Saviour lay in His father's shop and meddled only with carpenter's chips, the devil troubled Him not; now that He is to enter more publicly upon His mediatorship the tempter pierceth His tender soul with many sorrows by solicitation to sin." It is the same with us. So long as we move on quietly in our ordinary life he does not trouble himself to harm us; but when we rouse up to new consecration and new activity in God's service he pounces upon us and tries to destroy us. It is therefore in our times of greatest spiritual exaltation that we need to be most watchful. We learn here also that we may expect to endure temptation in this world. New power came to Jesus through His conflicts. His life was developed and made perfect through sufferings. Then He was fitted for sympathy with us in our temptations by Himself being tempted in all points as we are. Temptations resisted always bring new strength.   — J. R. MILLER

JUNE 19   *And David . . . behaved himself wisely. . . .*   —I Samuel 18:5

It would have been easy for David, fresh from h's victory over Goliath, to let all of this "go to his head." Actually, David won an even greater battle against himself and the pride to which he might have fallen victim. Many are at their best in the heat of battle — but are spoiled by success. So many spoil their victories by displaying them. In order to remain truly humble we must acknowledge our complete dependence upon God, whether it be in great victory or in the everyday experiences of life.

JUNE 20

So they called Rebekah and asked her, "Are you willing to go with this man?" Her answer was, "I will go!" —Genesis 24:58 Berkeley

Rebekah's act of faith in returning to Canaan to become the bride of Isaac is often forgotten. Yet, this young woman's stand was a courageous one, an uncompromising act of separation from her father's house and the familiar surroundings in which she had grown up. She voluntarily gives all of this up to marry someone she has never seen, someone about whom she knows very little. Her stand illustrates the position the young Christian must take if he is to be victorious in his new life. Isaac is a picture of the unseen Bridegroom, the One Whose we are and Whom we serve. If we are to be effective Christians, we must separate ourselves from everything which we might hold more dear, so that we might give ourselves whole-heartedly and completely into His service.

JUNE 21

The earnest (heartfelt, continued) prayer of a righteous man makes tremendous power available — dynamic in its workings. —James 5:16 Amplified

During a war between two countries in the Far East, one country was cleverly taken in by a Western power, which sold empty shells to its naive neighbor. When the day of battle arrived, this Far Eastern country found itself trying to fire empty shells. That is what many professed prayers become — empty shells. They have nothing in them and they accomplish nothing — because they lack "heart." "Heartfelt" prayer, on the other hand, exerts tremendous influence and power. Since we have such a great God, what great power our prayers *might* unloose if they were sincere and "earnest"! If you were God, would you listen to your prayers?

JUNE 22   *Go then and make disciples of all the nations. . . .*
—Matthew 28:19 Amplified

How old must one be before he can catch a glimpse of the missionary vision? James Elliot, at the age of 19, wrote, "Missionaries are very human folks, just doing what they are asked. Simply a bunch of nobodies trying to exalt Somebody."* Not too many years later, Jim gave his life obeying the command of Christ to "Go." True, not all of us *can* go in the sense that we depart for foreign shores with the message of the Gospel. But every Christian, no matter how young or ungifted, has the responsibility to obey this command to the best of his God-given ability, within the scope of God's will for his life. We, as Christians, are to "make disciples" or lead unbelievers to the only One who can help them to make the most important decision of their lives. We may be "nobodies," but we certainly are serving "Somebody" and obeying His command.

JUNE 23   *Love is of God; and every one that loveth is born of God, and knoweth God.*   —I John 4:7

We may, if we choose, make the worst of one another. Every one has his weak points; every one has his faults. We may make the worst of these; we may fix our attention constantly upon them. But we may also make the best of one another. We may forgive, even as we hope to be forgiven. We may put ourselves in the place of others, and ask what we should wish to be done to us, and thought of us, were we in their place. By loving whatever is lovable in those around us, love will flow back from them to us, and life will become pleasure instead of pain. — A. P. STANLEY

* From *Shadow of the Almighty* by Elisabeth Elliot. Used by permission of the publishers, Harper and Brothers, New York.

JUNE 24 *Whereby perceive we the love of God, because he laid down his life for us. . . .* —I John 3:16

The love of God is as broad in its expanse as the blue sky above. You can look up and appreciate, to a certain extent, the vastness of the sky — but human eyes cannot begin to measure its true extent. In much the same way, you can faintly comprehend the immensity of the sea, but only see part way into its unfathomable depths. The love of God is just as far beyond human understanding — but, thank God, you need not understand it to enjoy it!

JUNE 25 *What is man, that thou art mindful of him?* —Psalm 8:4

I stand at the foot of the mountain which lifts its head beyond the cloud and catches on its summit the first gleam of the King of Day in his rising, and I say, "What am I?" That mountain has been there through the passing of the ages, and I am here and shall be gone before the sun melts the snow upon its summit. "What is man?" But the Psalmist has another point of observation: "Thou art mindful of him; Thou visitest him." — G. CAMPBELL MORGAN

JUNE 26 *May grace (spiritual blessing) and peace be given you in increasing abundance. . . .* —I Peter 1:2 Amplified

These two words, *grace* and *peace,* contain in them the whole sum of Christianity. Grace contains the remission of sins; peace, a quiet and joyful conscience. When the grace and peace of God are in the heart, then is man strong. Then he can neither be cast down by adversity nor puffed up by prosperity, but walks on evenly, keeping to the highway. It is in the spirit that you find the paradise of grace and peace. — MARTIN LUTHER

JUNE 27

Sware by the Lord, the God of heaven and earth that you will not get my son a wife from the daughters of the Canaanites. . . . Instead, . . . (God) will send His angel ahead of you, so that you may obtain a wife from there for my son.

Genesis 24:3, 7 Berkeley

Mixed marriages must have been a problem in Abraham's day, as well as in this modern day. Abraham's God-given solution is still effective today — and God is still interested enough to delegate an angel as a match maker! Young people today should "think twice" before contemplating marriage outside of the family of God. Before choosing a life's mate, it would be God's best to limit "the field" to those of "like precious faith." Abraham and his servant realized the wisdom of this procedure, and the servant was willing to allow the angel to guide him in the final selection — just as God's young people today should not only look for God's guidance, but also be willing to wait patiently for Him. Those who walk ahead of God in this vital matter will find themselves outside of His will.

JUNE 28

Choose you this day whom ye will serve.

—Joshua 24:15

Destiny is fixed by the choice of the human will, which selects for itself its heaven or hell. Thus each one of us is building character forever. Those who are yielding to the forces around that mar the life do so absolutely of their own free choice. — G. CAMPBELL MORGAN

JUNE
29
. . . worship the LORD *in the beauty of holiness.*
—Psalm 29:2

An old but true adage says, "Beauty is as beauty does." If every Christian had a beautiful character, the cause of Christ would certainly advance with greater efficiency and impact. Too often, however, the Christian does not bear in his character the marks of true Christian beauty, as personified in the Lord Himself when He walked the Galilean countryside. True Christian graces are collected along the path of consecrated Christian living. If the Christian is not learning something new each day to help him in the important task of living the Christ-life, then he is no longer progressing but stagnant. And in the stagnant pool, new life is virtually eliminated. So let us as Christians be open to the life-giving power of the risen Christ.

JUNE
30
He that hath seen me hath seen the Father.
—John 14:9

God may be truly and experientially known through the Lord Jesus Christ Who is none other than the eternal Word become flesh, the very Deity incarnate in our humanity, the "Lamb slain from the foundation of the world," the only but all-sufficient Redeemer, Reconciler and Restorer of men to God. In Him alone, in Him directly and heart-satisfyingly, we may know the Creator-Spirit of the universe, and hold fellowship with Him as our heavenly Father. Our Lord Jesus said, "I am the way, the truth, and the life: no man cometh unto the Father but by Me." Later He added, "This is life eternal, that they might know thee the only true God, and Jesus Christ, whom thou hast sent." —J. SIDLOW BAXTER

JULY

We do not well. . . .   —II Kings 7:9

The four lepers who sat just outside the gate of Samaria, after they had come upon the spoil in the tents of the Syrians, passed on the "good news." They said one to another, "This day is a day of good tidings, and we hold our peace: if we tarry till the morning light, some mischief will come upon us: now therefore come, that we may go and tell the king's household." And the child of God who knows the "good tidings" of the Gospel "does not well" if he or she does not pass it on to others. Andrew came into contact with Jesus, and immediately he went to his brother Simon, and said: "We have found the . . . Christ. And he brought him to Jesus." Will you tell some hungry soul about Him today?
                                                        — M. R. DeHaan

And after He had dismissed the multitude, He went up into the hills by Himself to pray. When it was evening He was still there alone.
                                        —Matthew 14:23 Amplified

It seems to be natural for us as Christians to pray *up* to success, but to cease praying *in* success. This was not the case with Jesus. After one of His most striking miracles, that of feeding the five thousand, He felt an even greater need for prayer. As Jesus needed strength-giving time alone with His Father, we, too, require the spiritual sustenance to enable us to live the victorious, overcoming life in the face of increasing temptations and expanding evil. Also remember that in success the temptation to pride grows greater and greater. Humble dependence upon God in prayer, then, will put self in its proper place.

JULY
3

Thou shalt have no other gods before me.
—Exodus 20:3

This is the first of the ten commandments God gave to Moses — and, significantly, if it were kept, all of the other commandments would be kept in this one. If we put nothing before God, our obedience would be complete. But how many times we put other "gods" in God's place — money, ambition, pleasure, recreation, etc. and so often we put ourselves first. But the only way to true peace and heart satisfaction is the way of obedience to God.

JULY
4

We are (persecuted and hard driven,) pursued, but not deserted — to stand alone; we are struck down to the ground, but never struck out and destroyed.
—II Corinthians 4:9 Amplified

There is an interesting parallel here with the modern game of baseball; a player is not out even though a strike or two has gone over the plate. Neither is a child of God struck out, even though there are strikes against him. On this day commemorating the Declaration of Independence, it is profitable to think of the *attitude* of our courageous forefathers. In the game of life, a defeated attitude leads to defeat. On the other hand, a positive outlook leads to victory. Think back to the passage of the children of Israel through the Red Sea. Seemingly, they had been struck out and there was no way to escape — until they looked up and received God's direction to go through the Red Sea. You and I as Christians must reach this point of yieldedness to God's direction before God can lead us according to His purpose and plan.

JULY 5   *And God said, . . . I will establish my covenant with him, (Isaac) for an everlasting covenant and with his seed after him.*   —Genesis 17:19

This is one of the first Messianic prophecies in the Bible, for God here refers to the Lord Jesus Christ as "the seed of Isaac" according to the flesh. Jesus was born a Jew and received His human form from the descendants of Isaac. The "covenant" mentioned here was fulfilled at the cross and the blessings incorporated in the covenant were extended to all men who would receive Him through the resurrection, the event commemorated as Easter Sunday. When Jesus arose He made the blessings of this covenant available to all men who would believe. How complete and far-reaching is the plan of God!

JULY 6   *So everyone who hears these words of Mine and acts upon them — obeying them — will be like a sensible (prudent, practical, wise) man who built his house upon the rock.* —Matthew 7:24 Amplified

"No other foundation can any man lay than that is laid." This is the foundation called for in God's blueprint of salvation. Many well-meaning church people today have the mistaken idea that "good works" are the foundation on which the house of salvation is built. Participation in the physical outreach of church work has, in many cases, become the criterion on which eternal destiny is decided. In His Sermon on the Mount Jesus destroys this false foundation. He answers the common question, "Lord, Lord, have we not prophesied in Your Name, and driven out demons in Your Name, and done many mighty works in Your Name?" by saying, "I never knew you. Depart from Me." The first responsibility of the Christian is to build on the only adequate foundation, the Lord Jesus Himself. After this act of commitment comes the responsibilities of good works.

JULY 7   *Stand every morning to thank and praise the Lord. . . .*   —I Chronicles 23:30

A good day begins with God. A wise merchant would no more think of going to business without communion with Christ than of going to the store without coat or hat or shoes. I used to have a very poor watch, and I had to set it every morning in order that I might make from it a guess about the time of day. Our souls are poor time-pieces, utterly disordered; and every morning we need to set them by the Sun of Righteousness. Before we start off to work or school, we need to pray for patience.

— T. DeWitt Talmage

JULY 8   *He who possesses the Son has that life; he who does not possess the Son of God does not have that life.*   —I John 5:12 Amplified

Everyone knows that the physical breath of life was originally breathed into man at the creation — but physical life is not what John is talking about here. He is concerned with *spiritual, eternal* life. This life, too, is a gift of God. The supreme simplicity of this arrangement is the very point at which we stumble. How can anything so infinite in scope be wrapped up in such a plain package? To be sure, there are concepts in the Word which are, in many cases, beyond the understanding of men. But God has provided a window through which His people can look into the deep things of the Word. This window is the simple plan of salvation, the acceptance by faith of His Son. We should be thankful that salvation does not require intellectual understanding, but that it is so simple even a child can *know*, with assurance, that he is safe in the arms of the Eternal.

JULY
9

The Lord appeared to Abraham and said unto him . . . Be thou perfect. . . . And I will . . . be a God unto thee. . . .   —Genesis 17:1, 7

How impossible to obey would be the command of God, "Be thou perfect," without the enablement of His promise in verse 7, "I will . . . be a God unto thee. . . ." So often our efforts to live the Christian life fail simply because we assume the burden of our imperfection.

JULY
10

From everlasting to everlasting, thou art God.   —Psalm 90:2

Nothing is more restful to the heart of man than the sense of the eternity of God. The thought is utterly beyond our perfect comprehension, for the mind of man cannot grasp the thought of eternity. The very fact, however, of our inability to do so is the reason for the security we feel when we remember that God is Himself eternal.

— G. Campbell Morgan

JULY
11

On the ground of Your word, I will lower the nets [again].   —Luke 5:5 Amplified

Obedience is the key to success. Peter had fished all night without success — if he had disobeyed Jesus' command to let down his nets again, he would have remained unsuccessful. Along with the obedience Peter evidenced here came vision, for it was after this experience that Peter forsook his nets, his mundane earthly profession, to take up the divine profession of "fishing for men." Peter was not always obedient, however. One of the most tragic object lessons in the New Testament is found in Peter's disobedience. How marvelous it is, however, that Peter never lost the vision, even though it was sometimes clouded.

JULY 12   *David said moreover, the Lord that delivered me out of the paw of the lion and out of the paw of the bear, he will deliver me out of the hand of this Philistine.*   —I Samuel 17:37

Goliath was not David's first "impossible" foe. This courageous youth had won many victories before he faced Goliath on the field of battle, victories against equally great odds. And his battles weren't only against outward foes. Note David's reply to Eliab's taunt in verse 28. How self-possessed David was even as a youth. He had also conquered fear, for notice his brave stand against the giant Goliath. He was perfectly calm in his complete dependence upon God for victory. David had conquered another foe, unbelief, through his many experiences with God's faithfulness. If we, too, look upon our experiences in life as God's "school" for us, we will be much better equipped to live for Him!

JULY 13   *For every one who exalts himself will be humbled [that is, ranked below others who are honored or rewarded], and he who humbles himself [that is, keeps a modest opinion of himself and behaves accordingly] will be exalted — elevated in rank.*   —Luke 14:11 Amplified

What is your philosophy of life? The world around us idolizes the man with "push." The world seems to feel that a man cannot be successful unless he has been able to climb to the top of his profession, regardless of what he has done to others in his frantic haste to get there. The watchword of the Christian, on the other hand, is "pull." Instead of selfish and exclusive pushing ahead, the Christian has as his motto, "Bear ye one another's burdens. . . ."

JULY 14   *Remember now thy Creator, in the days of thy youth.*
—Ecclesiastes 12:1

Many times this verse has been expounded in messages to youth, but seldom has the rightful emphasis been placed on that little word, "now." It was the Apostle Paul who wrote, *"Now* is the accepted time, *Now* is the day of salvation. . . ."* Salvation is essential to life. A life lived apart from God is a life completely wasted. That is why it is so important that you make your decision for Christ early in life — *now* — so that your life might be used in *Christ's* service rather than in *self*-service. Don't give Him the shell, the dregs of your life! Give Him that which He purchased on Calvary, all of you!

JULY 15   *I know him that he . . . [and] his children . . . after him . . . shall keep the way of the Lord.*
—Genesis 18:19

God wants people that He can depend upon. He could say of Abraham, "I know him, that the Lord may bring upon Abraham all that He hath spoken." God can be depended upon; He wants us to be just as decided, as reliable, as stable. This is just what faith means. God is looking for men on whom He can put the weight of all His love, and power, and faithful promises. When God finds such a soul there is nothing He will not do for him. God's engines are strong enough to draw any weights we attach to them. Unfortunately the cable which we fasten to the engine is often too weak to hold the weight of our prayer. Therefore, God is drilling us, disciplining us, and training us to stability and certainty in the life of faith.

— A. B. SIMPSON

JULY 16   *Faith cometh by hearing, and hearing by the word of God.*   —Romans 10:17

Dwight L. Moody, one of the most remarkable men ever to live, and a man of great yet simple faith, said this, "I prayed for faith, and thought that some day faith would come down and strike me like lightning. But faith did not seem to come. One day I read in the tenth chapter of Romans, 'Now faith cometh by hearing, and hearing by the Word of God.' I had closed my Bible, and prayed for faith. I now opened my Bible and began to study, and faith has been growing ever since."   —BETTY CARLSON

JULY 17   *For you are all sons of light and sons of the day; we do not belong either to the night or to darkness.*   —I Thessalonians 5:5 Amplified

What a contrast in sound lies in the two words — light and darkness. The first seems to incorporate all that is bright and happy; it personifies what the Christian life really means. Its opposite, darkness, seems to express all that is mysterious and fiercesome, the blackness of eternity forever. How appropriate that we as Christians are called "sons of light" and have as our Saviour "the Father of light."

JULY 18   *And behold, the whole town went out to meet Jesus, and as soon as they saw Him, they begged Him to depart. . . .*   —Matthew 8:34 ANT

Generally, the common people of Jesus' day welcomed Him. Why did these people wish Him to depart? Bluntly, they were so concerned about a herd of pigs that they could not rejoice when a man's soul had been delivered from the domination of the devil. Even today, there are times when we as young people do not welcome Him because we are more concerned about material things than spiritual.

JULY
19
My soul followeth hard after thee. —Psalm 63:8

Often our lives are environed by things, gadgets, appliances until we have little time for God or friendships. We mortgage our future and deprive ourselves of peace of mind in order to gain the things which modern civilization dictates as essential to a full life. The soul that is following hard after God will be content with such things as he has. He will be happy with meager supplies, for he has the Owner of all things for his God and the Sustainer of the universe for his roommate.   — OLIVER G. WILSON

JULY
20
But even the very hairs of your head are all numbered.   —Matthew 10:30 Amplified

There are two aspects to this promise — comfort and warning. It is truly comforting to know that we as His children are so important to Him that He knows the most intimate details of our being, as our Creator certainly does. Sometimes, in our very "humanness," we cannot see the trees for the forest. We are blinded by the bigness of things and overlook the small details. God is not so limited. His vision includes the most minute detail along with the most gigantic of generalities. He knows each of His sheep "by name." It is comforting to know that we have a God of this caliber — but it is alarming when we realize how *well* God knows us. For with Him nothing is hidden. Be careful, then, in every area of your life, that in God's sight you will not be ashamed of its most minute detail. So live that when "your time comes" you may confidently rest, secure in God's care.

JULY 21

I am the Good Shepherd and I know and recognize My own, and My own know and recognize Me. —John 10:14 Amplified

These are the words of the soul's Shepherd. He knows His sheep as individuals, regardless of the fact that there are multitudes of His followers. In the physical sense the individual tends to become lost in the crowd. In this day of huge audiences numbering 100,000 and more, the individual completely loses his identity. Not so with God! Picture yourself in a crowd numbering in the millions — yet you stand out as an individual to your God. The blessing of this promise does not stop with the knowledge of our importance in God's sight. The gospel record adds that our soul's Shepherd is known and recognized by each one of His own. Ours is not an impersonal Sovereign, One to whom we dare not go with our everyday problems. Ours is a personal God whose ears are always open to our pleas.

JULY 22

I appeal to you therefore, brethren, and beg of you in view of [all] the mercies of God, to make a decisive dedication of your bodies — presenting all your members and faculties — as a living sacrifice. . . . —Romans 12:1 Amplified

God *wants* your body. Even more, He *needs* you. He wants to work in this world through the faculties He has given you — your brain, your eyes, your hands, your feet — every part of you. What is more, He wants your body as a *living* sacrifice. The prime of life is youth — that is why the greatest sacrifice you can make is that of your own strong "youthful" body — now, today! Once you look upon your body as God's gift and your "reasonable service" for Him, all the subtle temptations to sin will fall by the wayside in the wake of your consecrated service for Him. Your body is God's temple — treat it as such!

JULY 23

Enfolded in love, let us grow up in every way and in all things into Him, who is the Head, [even] Christ. . . .
—Ephesians 4:15 Amplified

Is it not a comfort to know that God in His rich mercy has not only gloriously saved us but made every provision for any repairs or adjustments that may be necessary along the way in our Christian life and testimony? His own wonderful grace is ours for the asking. The fulness of His blessed Holy Spirit is ours for the taking. He sends His own servants with the Word of Truth that we may be thoroughly furnished unto all good works and made to stand perfect and complete in all the will of God. Our God has done all to insure us a radiant effective life of service. *He has not failed us.* Dare we fail Him?

— MERRILL F. UNGER

JULY 24

And He (the Lord) replied, You must love the Lord your God with all your heart. . . .
—Luke 10:27 Amplified

Though this lawyer was trying to trap Christ with his question, "Teacher, what am I to do to inherit everlasting life?" still he had the right answer to Jesus' counter question, "What is in the law?" For the secret of life *is* found in our attitude toward God. Where does this love for God come from? Can we learn it or live it? Can we command it by an act of will? No, love is not a result of work on our part, it is a result of fruit in our lives from seed sown by God Himself. Fruit grows in suitable soil. Our part is to prepare the soil. God's part is to plant the seed. How do we prepare our life's soil for God's fruit to grow? By spending our time in His fellowship, by Bible study and prayer. As we walk with God, our love for Him will grow with constant communion.

JULY 25

For he that loveth another hath fulfilled the law.
—Romans 13:8

There are two ways of trying to lead the religious life — the way of law and the way of love. We may think of God and His will in terms of rules and regulations. This is prescribed; that is allowed; something else is forbidden. If we want to know how to be good we look it up in the Book. Thus did the Pharisees view religion. They believed that God had revealed the laws of the Bible, and religion and morality consisted in keeping those laws. Though that view of religion has produced great souls, it leads most men to formality and pride and self-righteousness.

But by the way of love we think of God, not as a law-giver, but as the Saviour. We regard Him, not as ordering and threatening us from outside, but as moving and molding us from within. He first loves us and, drawn by that love, we love Him; and in love to all our fellows we are drawn close to them and to Him.   — J. T. ADDISON

JULY 26

If we live, we live to the Lord and if we die, we die to the Lord. So then, whether we live or we die, we belong to the Lord.   —Romans 14:8 Amplified

What are you living for? What is most important to you? Many of us, if we had to answer this question, would have to say, "I live for popularity!" rather than, "I live for God." Popularity is our goal, the most important thing in our life. Others would have to admit that pleasures, luxury, and many other modern so-called "necessities" require their greatest efforts. The Apostle Paul said, "We belong to the Lord." By putting the Lord in His proper place in his life, Paul learned that the Christian life is lived in dimensions. Unless Christ is central in the Christian's life, it will be impossible for him to follow Christ as leader.

Bring my soul out of prison. . . . —Psalm 142:7

If you and I see the truth about Christ and then explain it to someone in our own dogmatic spirit, we are in this prison! Oswald Chambers says there soon appears "a smell of gunpowder" around this type of two-fisted saint. Said saint may be running around "evangelizing" but most likely the "fruit does not remain" because the hardhitting saint's own soul is in the prison of "having to be right." The love of God *melts*. He never uses a hammer. If your temper flares, if you are easily insulted or shocked, look around you carefully. You may be in prison and not know it. True humility, true meekness is not easily shocked or insulted. It does not flare. There is no aroma of "gunpowder" around true humility. Only the aroma of Christ.

—EUGENIA PRICE

In Him was Life. . . . —John 1:4 Amplified

"Live it up" is a common expression. Many make this their life's motto without fully understanding what is meant by this everyday expression. The very expression itself speaks of the brevity or limitations of earthly life. This life is something that can be "lived up," used up and exhausted. Looking to this earthly existence as an example of life is like visiting a hospital to see an example of health, or going to the town dump to find nature's beauty. True life is found only in Christ. This life alone is exhaustless, endless, without limitations. If you want to "live it up" then go to the Source of life, the One who alone can supply life, Jesus Christ.

JULY 29

For the Son of man is Lord [even] of the Sabbath.
—Matthew 12:8 Amplified

The Lord made this clear-cut statement to the strict Pharisees. They kept the Sabbath, it is true, but not out of a spirit of love. These legalistic fault-finders had questioned the Lord and His disciples for their "unlawful" Sabbath activities. Jesus' answer shows them that they have put the cart before the horse. If you do not live for the Lord because you love Him, your good and lawful life means nothing for eternity and little for today. But if you are motivated by love, even your mistakes will be covered and your failures forgiven. If you love the Lord with your whole heart, you may confidently expect Him to show you how best to live on His special day.

JULY 30

Everything that had breath and lived on dry land perished. . . . Only Noah and those with him in the ark remained alive.
—Genesis 7:22, 23 Berkeley

It is important to remember that the flood waters which drowned the wicked were the very waters which bore Noah and his family to safety. In the providence of God what may seem to be tragedies are often the very means which God uses to lead His children into a higher place of service or surrender. Just as Noah must have thanked God for deliverance *through* the flood, God's children today should remember to give thanks to Him for their deliverance *through* adversity. That tree which survives the greatest beating from wind and weather is the tree that becomes the hardiest and most rugged. This is true in the life of the Christian as well. God chastens those whom He loves. Seen in this light, difficulties become stepping stones to greater heights of Christian service.

JULY 31

If I [can] speak in the tongues of men and [even] of angels, but have not love [that reasoning, intentional, spiritual devotion such as is inspired by God's love for and in us], I am only a noisy gong . . . . —I Corinthians 13:1 Amplified

One of God's choicest servants, now with his Lord, Dr. Oliver G. Wilson, once wrote, "Practice the grace of giving up, the art of giving in, and the virtue of holding in." In this brief sentence he succeeded in summing up what should be the Christian's attitude toward his fellow men. That does not mean that a Christian young person should have no convictions or the backbone to stand up for them. It does mean that he should be so motivated by the love of God shining through him that his own desires, whether great or small, will not be placed before his desire that the unbelievers among whom he moves might become acquainted with his Saviour. Christians must be characterized by a spirit of love, even for those who heartily disagree with them.

AUGUST

AUG.
1

But seek for (aim at and strive after) first of all His kingdom, and His righteousness [His way of doing and being right], and then all these things taken together will be given you besides.
—Matthew 6:33 Amplified

Everyone enjoys a shopping trip, but how foolish one would be if he returned from his shopping spree, unwrapped his purchases, threw the merchandise in the wastebasket and kept the wrappings! Yet that is what many Christians today are doing in the spiritual sense. "Wrappings" such as popularity, cars, etc. have become, in the lives of many of us, more important than eternal goods.

AUG.
2

Let not sin therefore rule as king in your mortal bodies.
—Romans 6:12 Amplified

The Christian should have an appetite for prayer. He should want to pray. One does not have to force food upon a healthy child. Exercise, good circulation, health and labor demand food for sustenance. So it is with those who are spiritually healthy. They have an appetite for the Word of God and for prayer. Sin breaks fellowship with God. A little girl committed a certain offense and when her mother discovered it she began to question her daughter. Immediately the child lost her smile and a cloud darkened her face as she said, "Mother, I don't feel like talking." So it is with us when our fellowship with God is broken by sin in our lives. We do not feel like talking to Him. If you do not feel like praying, it is probably a good indication that you should start praying immediately.
—BILLY GRAHAM

AUG.
3
The prayer of the upright is His delight.
—Proverbs 15:8 Berkeley

What the church needs today is not more machinery or better, not new organizations or more and novel methods, but men whom the Holy Ghost can use — men of prayer, men mighty in prayer. The Holy Ghost does not flow through methods, but through men. He does not come on machinery, but on men. He does not anoint plans, but men — men of prayer. — E. M. BOUNDS

AUG.
4
When Abraham learned that his kinsman (Lot) had been captured he . . . marched in pursuit. . . . brought back his kinsman Lot. . . .
—Genesis 14:14, 16 Berkeley

What an example of "brotherly" love and concern we find in Abraham's generous "heart" action in behalf of his wayward relative, Lot. So often we lack genuine concern about the spiritual condition of our relatives and friends. Our prayer should be that God would lay hold upon our hearts a heavy burden for these loved ones and show us how to lead them to the Saviour.

AUG.
5
The people who sat (dwelt enveloped) in darkness have seen a great Light, and for those who sat in the land and shadow of death Light has dawned.
—Matthew 4:16 Amplified

Manned lighthouses are rapidly becoming a rarity in this modern day, but if you have ever seen a lighthouse in action you will have noticed how the area immediately surrounding the base of the lighthouse was left dark and dismal. This should not be the case for the Christian, but too often, it is at home that our Christian witness suffers. The solution is found in a closer touch with the Lord through His Word and prayer.

AUG.
6
Cain rose up against Abel his brother, and slew him. —Genesis 4:8

On the top of a hill in a midwestern state stands a courthouse so situated that raindrops falling on one side of the roof travel by way of the Great Lakes into the Atlantic, while drops on the opposite side find their way through the Ohio and Mississippi to the Gulf. Just a breath of wind one way or another may determine whether a single raindrop will end up either in the Gulf or in the Atlantic. Even so, one single decision is enough to determine man's destiny, either heaven or hell. Have you made the right decision? — M. R. DeHaan

AUG.
7
The Lord said to Abraham . . . leave your land. . . . So Abraham took his departure as the Lord had told him. . . . —Genesis 12:1, 4 Berkeley

There is a lesson here for young people in particular — a lesson in prompt obedience. Even though the Lord's command meant that Abraham must leave his wealth and loved ones at an age when it would be difficult for him to start over (he was 75 years old), yet he obeyed without hesitation. In fact, there is almost a note of joy in the record of his departure. If all of us as God's children would obey the commands of the Lord as unhesitatingly, we would not only please God, but we would find great joy and satisfaction in such action. A thought for the day — be as prompt in obedience as you are in complaining!

AUG.
8

It is no longer I who live, but Christ, the Messiah, lives in me. . . . —Galatians 2:20 Amplified

A little girl, applying for membership in a church, was asked by the pastor what she thought it would mean for her to be a Christian. She replied, "I suppose it will be to do what Jesus would do, and to behave as Jesus would behave if He were a little girl and lived at our house." There could be no better definition of a consecrated life. We are always to ask, "What would Jesus do?" and then try to do the same. A Christian is always a Christian, wherever he may go. He is never off duty. He always represents Christ. He must always strive to be what Jesus would be, and do what Jesus would do in his place.

— J. R. MILLER

AUG.
9

As you have therefore received the Christ, [even] Jesus the Lord, [so] walk — regulate your lives and conduct yourselves — in union with and conformity to Him. —Colossians 2:6 Amplified

Just as it is much easier to keep a fire burning than to rekindle it after it has gone out, so it is easier simply to continue in a proper habit than it is to change one's habits. This is true in the spiritual realm as well. The ancient Greeks maintained what they called the sacred fire, never allowing it to go out; in a higher sense, we as Christians should keep the heavenly flame aglow in our hearts. A proper spiritual habit once formed becomes the normal reaction of our lives — but these proper spiritual habits do not begin without effort on our part. We do not become channels of the Spirit until we have undergone a thorough cleansing by the Spirit.

AUG.
10
Pray the Lord of the harvest to force out and thrust laborers into His harvest. . . . Jesus sent out these twelve. . . .—Matthew 9:38; 10:5 Amplified

Evidently the prayers of these disciples were answered very pointedly and abruptly — by their being sent out themselves. Such a contingency might well be the result of any sincere prayer on the part of one of God's children. That is why sincere prayer is, in a sense, very dangerous for the believer. For who knows which one of His children God will choose to carry out His program, whether it be on the foreign mission field or in some routine position in the homeland? When you pray for the Lord to thrust out laborers into the harvest, are you willing to be one of those who will be sent? That is a question each must answer honestly in the affirmative if he is to pray effectively and "in the spirit."

AUG.
11
To all that be in Rome, beloved of God, called to be saints.
—Romans 1:7

The meaning of the word "saint" is exactly the same as "sanctify." True sainthood is Christian sanctification or separation — separation from our unregenerate past, from worldliness, from all known sinful ways; and separatedness to an outward confession of Christ, and an inward fellowship with Christ, and a daily usableness by Christ. The first business of every Christian is this sanctification, or separatedness, and the development of holy character. This is not incompatible with legitimate employment in business, unless our occupation itself is wrong. We can make all our circumstances contribute, if we will, to the furtherance of real sainthood. This is the highest of all callings; and this is the supreme glory of the Christian life.

— J. SIDLOW BAXTER

AUG.
12
It will be difficult for a rich man to get into the kingdom of heaven. —Matthew 19:23 Amplified

What is the nature of true riches? The rich man whose *only* wealth is counted in *material* things is certainly poorer than the poor man who counts his wealth only in spiritual things. "Money talks" — but not in eternity. The younger we are when we learn this lesson, the greater will be our spiritual enrichment. There is nothing evil about material things — the evil lies in our attitude toward these *things*. If we place primary importance upon the things of God, we need not worry about our material possessions standing in the way of our spiritual destination.

AUG.
13
Do not gather and heap up and store for yourselves treasures on earth . . . But gather and heap up and store for yourselves treasures in heaven. . . .
—Matthew 6:19, 20 Amplified

It must grieve the heart of God as He sees His children exhausting themselves in the mad rush to accumulate things. It must arouse His derisive laughter to watch men scramble for those things which moth and rust can corrupt and destroy. "Only those things which are done for Christ will last," the poet points out. And this is truly a Scriptural position. One does not need to look far to see evidences of the destructive force of time operating on the "things" of earth. Nothing man-made lasts — only those activities and donations in the realm of Christian service have any lasting value in results that are handed down from generation to generation. We as Christian young people must see as God sees and place the proper value and emphasis on eternal things.

AUG.
14

Who is she that looketh forth as the morning, fair as the moon, clear as the sun?

—Song of Solomon 6:10

As you know, the moon itself is a *dead planet*. It only has light and heat as it reflects the sun. So, too, we only have light and joy and spiritual warmth as we reflect the Lord Jesus Christ.

The only time the moon does not shine is when there is an eclipse; that is, when the earth comes between the sun and the moon. In like manner, when there is lack of joy and victory in our life, or when there is spiritual coldness, it is usually due to the fact that the "world" has come between us and the Lord. — H. G. BOSCH

AUG.
15

You are the salt of the earth, but if salt has lost its taste — its strength, its quality — how can its saltness be restored? —Matthew 5:13 Amplified

The chemical formula for salt reveals that this basic element is made up of two components: One, sodium, is an unstable, metallic substance; the other, chlorine, is a gas with strong bleaching power. Man's natural, carnal, earthly character is like sodium, unstable and irresponsible; on the other hand, the Holy Spirit embodies the gaseous, bleaching characteristics of chlorine. When the Holy Spirit enters the young person's heart, He makes the difference. He is the difference between the natural or carnal and the spiritual. Man without Christ is like salt which has lost its taste, strength, quality. Ever since his fall at the dawn of Creation, man has been incomplete outside of Christ. Only as Christ, through the Holy Spirit, assumes His rightful place in man, does man regain the perfect position that was His, fresh from the creative act of God.

AUG.
16
Then Jesus answered her, O woman, great is your faith! Be it done for you as you wish.
—Matthew 15:28 Amplified

Jesus seemed strangely reluctant to answer this woman's plea for her demon-possessed daughter (verses 22 - 27). He makes it clear that His ministry is only to His own people, the Jews. Yet, because of her faith, the Lord answered her prayer. It is encouraging for us to remember that, as someone has said, "Prayer is not conquering God's reluctance but laying hold of God's willingness." If we really believed this, our prayer life would be much more vital and meaningful. We would not hesitate to lay before the Lord every concern of ours no matter how minor. Our fellowship with Him would be close and constant — and as a result, our lives would reflect Him more clearly.

AUG.
17
Whether therefore ye eat, or drink, or whatsoever ye do, do all to the glory of God.
—I Corinthians 10:31

This must ever be our guiding principle of action in all matters, but especially in that most vital issue of our relationship to God's will and our adjustment to God's plan. God is glorified when we make known to a lost world the glories of His grace, the wonders of His salvation in Christ, and the blessings of faith in His Word and His will. His plan for each life provides for the maximum degree of usefulness in this holy service. When we find and enter into God's plan we thus glorify Him most. His glory, moreover, means blessing to men and benefit to ourselves. Men are never more helped than by a yielded Spirit-filled believer who makes Christ known to them. We ourselves are never more blessed than when blessing our fellowman and thus glorifying God.   — MERRILL F. UNGER

AUG.
18

When John in prison heard about the activities of Christ, he sent a message by his disciples and asked Him, Are You He Who was to come, or should we keep on expecting a different one?
—Matthew 11:2, 3 Amplified

Can this be the same John the Baptist who confidently presented Jesus as "the Lamb of God which taketh away the sin of the world"? John's prison experience must have caused him to doubt, but he expressed his doubt to the right Person — the Lord Jesus. And Jesus has a simple, unassailable answer, in essence, "What I am doing shows Who I am." Every one of my doubts, and it is normal for me to doubt, is answered in the Person of Christ. My faith, if it is anchored in the Rock, may be shaken but it can never be uprooted! Remember John when you face doubts and take your doubts to the same One!

AUG.   *I will lift up my eyes. . . .*   —Psalm 121:1
19

Some years ago the late Lord Northcliffe of England, editor and owner of *The London Times,* was threatened with complete blindness. His eyes were examined by specialists, but nothing essentially wrong with them could be found. The specialists concluded that he needed the "far look." He had been using his eyes too much for reading fine print and for close observation. He was advised to take days in the country away from the printed pages where he could look on the vast horizons of God's creation. The simple remedy corrected the great man's eye trouble. Many of God's dear children are in serious danger of becoming spiritually blind by the continued viewing of the near — the problems close at hand, a narrow span of interests, resulting in a sort of spiritual astigmatism.

— OLIVER G. WILSON

AUG.
20

If you have faith — a firm relying trust — and do not doubt, you will not only do what has been done to the fig tree, but even if you say to this mountain, Be taken up and cast into the sea, it will be done. —Matthew 21:21 Amplified

A faith that moves mountains? In this day of tremendous mechanical achievements and great scientific advances, a simple faith, a "relying" trust in God, is a rare thing. Today man's faith rests in man's achievements, rather than in God's provision. Thus, we place a limitation on God that exists only in ourselves. God is limitless.

AUG.
21

And while he lingered, the men laid hold upon his hand, and upon the hand of his wife, and upon the hand of his two daughters, the Lord being merciful unto him: and they brought him forth, and set him without the city. —Genesis 19:16

What a picture of God's mercy! First, He warned Lot, of what was going to happen to Sodom and Gomorrah. Then, as Lot hesitated, God sent angels to lead him out of the city. Still Lot was reluctant to leave, and ultimately the angels had to force him from the surroundings he had come to love. Why was God so merciful to Lot, particularly in the face of his stubborn desire to remain in the city of wickedness? Why did not God abandon him to suffer the same fate as the unbelievers? That is a question that could be asked not only in Lot's case, but also in ours. What have we done to merit God's attention and mercy? Why should we be saved, while scores of those around us are taking the broad way to destruction? The answer is found in our attitude toward God and His attitude toward us. Lot, despite his failings, was a believer; we, too, are believers. We cannot understand it, but we can, we *must*, believe it by faith.

AUG. 22

We have waited for him, and He will save us: this is the Lord; we have waited for him, we will be glad and rejoice in his salvation. —Isaiah 25:9

Do not be discouraged at your faults; bear with yourself in correcting them as you would with your neighbor. Lay aside this ardor of mind which exahusts your body and leads you to commit errors. Accustom yourself gradually to carry prayer into all your daily occupations. Speak, move, and work in peace, as if you were in prayer, as indeed you ought to be. Do everything without excitement, by the spirit of grace. As soon as you perceive your natural impetuosity gliding in, retire quietly within, where is the kingdom of God. Listen to the leadings of grace; then say and do nothing but what the Holy Spirit shall put in your heart. You will find that you will become more tranquil, that your words will be fewer and more effectual, and that, with less effort, you will accomplish more good.

— FRANCOIS DE LA MOTHE FENELON

AUG. 23

You are my friends, if you keep on doing the things which I command you to do.
—John 15:14 Amplified

It was the patriarch Abraham who was called "the friend of God." What was the basis of this friendship? It was Abraham's obedience by faith to the demands and commands of God. What more wonderful designation could a man have than to be known as "a friend of God!" Jesus Himself delighted in His earthly friendships. He surrounded Himself with close companions when He walked on earth. With His friends He shared all the riches at His disposal. And these were true riches — the riches of the Spirit. He wants to be your Friend, your Confidant. No earthly pal could be as wonderful a companion as He!

AUG.
24
Then the Lord asked Cain, Where is your brother Abel? He said, "I do not know, am I my brother's keeper?"
—Genesis 4:9 Berkeley

In the program of God, each blood-bought child has a definite responsibility to those who are still without Christ. True, we as Christians can not "convert" men. All we can do to fulfill our responsibilities as Christians is to make sure that the light of God's love shines brightly through us and is not dimmed by any dark clouds of sin or doubt in our lives. In that sense, we *are* our brother's keeper. If we cause another to stumble on the path of life by some inconsistency or failure in our Christian life, we will be held accountable. All we can do is cast ourselves upon God's grace and mercy, asking Him first of all to cleanse our lives, and then to use them.

AUG.
25
Be glad and supremely joyful. . . . when people revile you and persecute you. . . .
—Matthew 5:12, 11 Amplified

This is a big order — a command from the lips of Christ Himself, one which seems impossible to carry out. The Christian life is a paradox — prescribing victory in surrender, loftiness in humility, greatness in smallness. The Lord measures stature not in feet and inches, but in surrender and humility. The average person rebels against such self-denial. Even the dedicated Christian remains susceptible to the temptation of pride. "I" is the central letter in this word "pride" — and "I" is the most dangerous enemy the Christian must face. Thus, this command of Christ to rejoice and be glad under persecution is really the heart of the Christian code — and it is a command impossible of fulfillment aside from the strength and ability Christ alone can provide.

AUG.
26
Be strong in the Lord and in the power of his might. —Ephesians 6:10

There are two ways of viewing the Christian life — the way of commandments and the way of communion. We may think of Jesus as a wonderful teacher who lived a noble life more than nineteen hundred years ago. He becomes our model and we strive to improve ourselves by copying Him and obeying His laws. Our motto then is: "Be strong like the Lord in the power of our own might." But there is another way. By it we realize that we cannot be saved by rules or models, but only by the personal and present force of the living Christ working, not outside us as a copy, but within us as a companion. We are not merely followers of Christ, but members of Christ through whom He expresses Himself, even as we use our own hands and eyes. Our motto then is: "Be strong *in* the Lord and in the power of His might," for He fills us, expanding and directing our powers. The Christian life is thus not a life of commandments but of companionship. Christ does not stand at the head of the stairs to watch us pull ourselves up. He stands at the door of our hearts and knocks. — A. T. ADDISON

AUG.
27
Behold now, this city is near to flee unto, and it is a little one: Oh, let me escape thither, (is it not a little one?) and my soul shall live. —Genesis 19:20

How longsuffering and patient God must be! Here He was leading Lot and his family away from the certain destruction of Sodom and Gomorrah, and Lot dares to question God's escape route! Lot had the audacity to dictate to God. Rather than being thankful to God for His deliverance, Lot tries to run his own life. Aren't many of us guilty of the same audacity?

AUG.
28
Love endures long and *is patient and kind.*
I Corinthians 13:4 Amplified

Napoleon is reported to have said: "Alexander, Caesar, Charlemagne and myself founded empires on force, and they perished; Jesus of Nazareth alone, a crucified Jew, founded His kingdom on love, and at this hour millions of men are ready to die for Him." The names of Hitler, Mussolini, Stalin, Khrushchev could be added to Napoleon's list of dictators, and still his conclusion would be correct . Yet how many Christians truly are ready to die for their faith? How many are willing to let their lights shine in love? We should search our hearts to ascertain our own willingness to stand and live for the right.

AUG.
29
Our God whom we serve. . . .
—Daniel 3:17

What a magnificent opportunity God in His providence created for these young men to bear witness for Him. They had been brought from Jerusalem as captives into Babylon. During their exile the law of the land commanded them to do what they knew to be wrong in the sight of God, or, in default, to be thrown into a burning fiery furnace. But in what attitude do we find them? We follow them in imagination to the great tribunal of the King of Babylon and hear their reply to his question, "Who is that God that shall deliver you out of my hands?" We almost fancy the three Hebrews to be the apostles of our Lord, and that they were acting upon the counsel which He gave — "When they deliver you up, take no thought how or what ye shall speak . . . for it is not ye that speak, but the Spirit of your Father which speaketh in you." We hear them saying: "O Nebuchednezzar, we are not careful to answer thee in this matter; if it be so, our God whom we serve is able to deliver us from the burning fiery furance." They did not know that He would, but they knew that He could, and that was sufficient for them. He was their God whom they served, and as He was almighty, they had nothing to fear. Can we this day call their God ours? And do we delight to serve Him? Oh, that it may be our meat and drink to do His blessed will! — JOHN ROBERTS

**AUG.
30**
And he . . . chose him five smooth stones out of the brook . . . and his sling was in his hand: and he drew near to the Philistine. —I Samuel 17:40

Why *"five"*? . . . Was not David a man of faith? Did he doubt that God would direct him and give him perfect timing and aim as he hurled the stone out of his trusty sling at the enemy of the Lord? Certainly he needed only one. But wait, did you know that Goliath had four brothers? (II Samuel 21:15-22) Knowing that they might rally to Goliath's defense, even if the rest of the Philistines did not, David was ready for them. He had great faith; one stone for Goliath, and one for each of his brothers was all that he needed. — H. G. BOSCH

**AUG.
31**
But the Word of God is not chained or imprisoned! —II Timothy 2:9 Amplified

Today man sees all his hopes and aspirations crumbling before him. He is perplexed and knows not whither he is drifting. But he must realize that the Bible is his refuge, and the rallying point for all humanity. It is here man will find the solution of his present difficulties and guidance for his future action. Unless he accepts with clear conscience the Bible and its great message, he cannot hope for salvation. For my part, I glory in the Bible.
— HAILE SELASSIE, *Emperor of Ethiopia*

SEPTEMBER

SEPT.
1

But what comes out of the mouth comes from the heart and this is what makes a man unclean and defiles [him]. . . . eating with hands unwashed does not make him unclean or defile [him].
—Matthew 15:18, 20 Amplified

Ours is a day of germ consciousness. On every side we are reminded of the importance of cleanliness and good hygiene habits. Unfortunately, we are emphasizing concern with the external at the expense of the internal. We seem to be overly concerned with unwashed hands and completely unconcerned about unwashed hearts. On the other hand, God was so concerned with the condition of men's hearts that He sent His Son to provide the means of cleansing the heart. As far as He is concerned, unwashed hearts exclude the individual from fellowship with Him. We as Christians should place greater emphasis on inner preparation for spiritual blessing — and pay less attention to outward appearances.

SEPT.
2

For God so loved the world. . . .   —John 3:16

We cannot know or enjoy or love the world too much, if God's will controls us. Has a mother anything but joy in watching her little daughter's devotion to her doll? Not until the child is so absorbed that she cannot hear her mother's voice. Did anyone ever love the world (it's people) more than Jesus did? Yet was anyone ever so loyal to the Father's will? Worldliness is not love of the world, but slavishness to it.   — M. D. BABCOCK

SEPT.
3
Set your minds and keep them set on what is above — the higher things — not on the things that are on the earth. —Colossians 3:2 Amplified

Our national tendency in this day seems to be toward a lowering of standards, as individuals and as a nation. In business, ethics no longer seem to have a place. The philosophy seems to be, "It is all right as long as you don't get caught at it!" The same philosophy seems to apply to the individual's moral conduct. Even in the realm of theology, there is a distinct tendency toward "watering down" spiritual precepts. What is the answer? We as young people should take our stand uncompromisingly in every area of life, determined not to let down any barriers but to maintain the standards which God, in His Word, has set up.

SEPT.
4
As He was walking by the sea of Galilee, He noticed two brothers . . . they were fishermen. —Matthew 4:18 Amplified

It is significant that Jesus called His first disciples from humble work in a humble walk of life — fishermen. Why didn't He go first to the colleges and seminaries of His day for men to teach? As J. H. Jowett once said, "There is nothing like plain glass for letting in the light!" What he meant is that higher learning is apt to become proud and arrogant, disdaining the simplicity of the Gospel. There is no room in an already filled pail. If one is filled with self-importance, he cannot make room for the things of the Spirit. "Except you become as little children," Jesus said, "you cannot enter the kingdom of God." This does not mean that we are not to take advantage of the opportunities for higher learning — but we *must* use intellectual advantage as a means of glorifying God rather than self.

SEPT.
5

We must obey God rather than men.
—Acts 5:29 Amplified

Without question the unplanned life is a tragedy. God has made His plan for us; we should make our plans to conform to His. We plan everything else — our education, our homes, our household duties, our social affairs. The captain of the ship moves by chart; the mountain climber employs a guide; the tourist follows his map or bluebook. The architect plans his house in every detail before he starts work. The painter plans his picture and every stroke of the brush is full of meaning. But too often the life itself is unplanned. The Bible tells us of a foolish man who began building a house without having counted the cost, and the house was a failure — it was never completed. Do we want to imitate that man? It is most unwise to leave God out of our planning.   — A. T. Rowe

SEPT.
6

And He said to them, Come after Me. . . . At once they left their nets and became His disciples.
—Matthew 4:19, 20 Amplified

This kind of prompt and ready obedience is hard to find these days, not only in obedience to God, but also in obedience to earthly parents. It is discouraging for an earthly parent to have to repeat a command over and over again. How much more it must grieve the heart of God when His children hesitate at His commands, never responding "immediately" or "at once" to carry out His will. Why not try carrying out God's commands *now!* You will find that He will help you do it and that life will take on a new meaning as you strive for His "Well done!"

SEPT.
7
. . . all things work together and are (fitting into a plan) for good to those who love God. . . .
—Romans 8:28 Amplified

The young person who has never known hardship, who never has had to practice self-denial or make a personal sacrifice, may be the envy of other young people whose lives have been one continued struggle. They may think that if they could have had his easy circumstances they could have made a great deal more of their lives. But in reality, their chance in life thus far has been much better than his. Manhood is made in the field of struggle and hardship, not in ways of ease and luxury. Hindrances are opportunities. Difficulty is a school for manhood.

— J. R. MILLER

SEPT.
8
I have overcome the world.
—John 16:33

This is the "world," in the morally evil sense, through which Satan seduces souls away from God. It is just as alluringly attractive as it is deceptively destructive. Millions are overcome by it. But there was One who, although tempted by it as no other, rode over it in absolute triumph, thereby breaking its power over all who become savingly united to Him. It is HE who says in our text, "I have overcome the world!" With Him indwelling us, we too may overcome; for "greater is He that is in you than he that is in the world" (I John 4:4). Our history books have told us that Alexander the Great overcame the world and then sat down and "wept because there were no more worlds to conquer." Actually, he was overcome *by* the world. He died prematurely, after a drunken debauch. The true victor and hero is the man who overcomes *the world* within himself.
— J. SIDLOW BAXTER

Who shall ever separate us from Christ's love?
—Romans 8:35 Berkeley

The Roman church, to whom Paul was writing, was facing persecution and was on the verge of a veritable scourging at the hands of the enemies of the Church of Jesus Christ. Paul became specific and mentioned some of the experiences which would fall to the lot of the Roman Christians — suffering, affliction, tribulation, calamity, distress, persecution, hunger, destitution, peril, and finally the sword. All of these eventually would become the experiences of these early Christians in Rome, and the historians of the day record for us their almost unbelievable courage in the face of torture and terrible death. One of the reasons they were able to hold their heads high was that they could speak Paul's inspired words, "We are more than conquerors . . . through Him who loved us."

Abstain from all appearance of evil.
—I Thessalonians 5:22

A good rule to follow in regard to questionable things, not specifically forbidden in the Word of God, is to leave them alone. That is the safe course to follow. The late Dr. H. A. Ironside tells the following story which will illustrate this truth.

Sandy was a thrifty Scot who, in order to save laundry expense, would wear the same shirt several times. On one occasion when dressing for a banquet he took a used shirt from the drawer. Not being sure of its cleanness, he held it up before the window to better examine it. His wife, Jean, noticing him shaking his head with indecision, called out, "Remember, Sandy, if it's doubtful, it's dirty!" Yes, if it's doubtful, it's dirty!　　　　— M. R. DeHaan

SEPT.
11
Whatsoever ye do, do it heartily as to the Lord.
—Colossians 3:23

I was talking to a salesman the other day, and he was discouraged because he was making only fair sales. He said, "It's so hard for me to sell these tires. I'm not genuinely sold on them myself."

A lot of us call ourselves Christians, but we make poor salesmen because we readily give the impression we're not genuinely sold ourselves. A basic Christian teaching is this: "Whatsoever ye do, do it heartily, as to the Lord, and not unto men." Paul, who wrote that, did not sit around and only write letters telling other people what they should and should not do. Everything he taught, he attempted to put into practice. I am sure he would be the first to admit that he fell on his face a few times. He lived very much of an overcoming sort of life; but what delights me about Paul — he did all things heartily unto His Lord.

— BETTY CARLSON

SEPT.
12
The Lord is good, a stronghold in the day of trouble; He knows those who commit themselves to Him.
—Nahum 1:7 Berkeley

The phrase, "The Lord is good," often appears in Scripture, being found in some of the most unlikely places throughout the Old Testament. Here in this prophecy (Nahum) of the fall of a great city, the writer cannot overlook this essential quality of the great Jehovah God. Even in the midst of chaos, "God is good." In our own troubled day, it is comforting to be able to rely on One who never changes, who "is the same yesterday, today and forever!" If we place our trust in Him, we can do no better, we can find no firmer stronghold, no stronger foundation. Who else can we trust in the world around us?

SEPT.
13
Lot took a good look and saw how well watered the whole Jordan district was. . . . So Lot chose the whole Jordan basin for himself.
—Genesis 13:10, 11 Berkeley

How superficial Lot's examination must have been. Apparently, he did not even walk over the land which he chose. One wonders if his selection was influenced by the prosperous cities that lay on the plain. Abraham, on the other hand, allowed God to choose for him, and Abraham's choice still remains the best to this very day, thousands of years after he made it. Lot, on the contrary, saw his choice demolished, almost before his eyes, leaving him destitute and dependent upon Abraham's charity toward him. What a lesson there is for young people in this account.

SEPT.
14
. . . in quietness and in confidence shall be your strength.
—Isaiah 30:15

The sign was as plain as could be: "Shoes Repaired While You Wait." But I walked right by, even though a nail in my shoe was annoying me with persistence. "No time now for repairs." So I hobbled on. My devotions were hurried and formal. The thought kept pressing upon me, "You must hurry. So much to do. Read but a verse and offer a short prayer." In my frenzied haste, I opened my Bible at random for a short portion of Scripture. There it was standing out before me as plain as the flashing signals at the railroad crossing: "They that wait upon the Lord shall renew their strength." "Repairs While You Wait." Not my old shoes, but my badly beaten spirit. Fuss, noise, bustle, expert efficiency, time-clock precision, all shout: "Haste!" We limp on, enduring, endeavoring, wearing ourselves to a frazzle. We need to wait for repairs.

— OLIVER G. WILSON

SEPT.
15
. . . I shall be anointed with fresh oil.—Psalm 92:10

The story is told of an enterprising shop-keeper who opened a shop right next door to another and handled the same goods. Spurred by the new competition the old established store-keeper put a sign over his shop painted in big letters, "ESTABLISHED FIFTY YEARS. PROVEN MERCHANDISE." The next day his competitor displayed a sign, "ESTABLISHED YESTERDAY, NO OLD STOCK." The only way to keep our life fresh is a daily anointing with fresh oil, as we study His Word, seek His will and witness for Him (Isaiah 40:31). — M. R. DeHaan

SEPT.
16
Be wary and wise . . . be innocent . . . be on guard . . . be brought . . . be hated . . . be saved. . . .
—Matthew 10:16, 17, 18, 20 Amplified

Here is a whole hive of "be's" — a sermon covering the whole gamut of the Christian experience in just a few sentences. The first step, wisdom, is "taking" — salvation is accepted as the free gift of God by grace. Innocence or freedom from the guilt of sin comes with the second step. An awareness of dangers from without is a sign of a maturing Christian. Then comes persecution, "being brought" for His name's sake into dangers. Then, as our witness shines clear in the midst of a "wicked and perverse generation," we will be subjected to hatred, but at the same time will be given the words to speak through the Holy Spirit. Ultimately, praise God, we will be saved because of our faithfulness unto God. These are just a few of the words Jesus spoke. How full of meaning and reality were the thoughts He expressed out of His earthly experience and heavenly wisdom!

If Jesus was tempted, then we may expect to be tempted, too. How encouraging for us to know that "we have not a high priest which cannot be touched with the feeling of our infirmities," because when He was upon the earth as "Son of Man" He was "in all points tempted like as we are." And during His temptations in the wilderness He was tempted to distrust, presumption, worldly ambition, and idolatry. It was a temptation, first, to distrust: "If Thou be the Son of God, command that these stones be made bread." It was a temptation also to presumption: "Cast thyself down" (from the pinnacle of the Temple), "for it is written, he shall give his angels charge concerning thee." Then it was a temptation to worldly ambition and idolatry: "All these things will I give thee if thou wilt fall down and worship me." A temptation to worship the devil! Perhaps there is no temptation that can possibly come to us from the evil one which cannot be reduced to one or another of these four temptations. But for our encouragement, as well as instruction, we are not only told that our Lord did conquer the great adversary, but also the way in which He achieved His victory. It was by using "the sword of the Spirit, which is the Word of God." To each temptation our Lord replied: "It is written." Let us learn and resolve from our meditation this day to become more and more familiar with the Word of God, and seek for grace to obey all its precepts. Then, if God permits either trial or temptation to cross our path, we shall come away "more than conquerors through Him that loved us."

— JOHN ROBERTS

SEPT.
18

I will set My bow in the clouds; it shall be a token of a covenant between Me and the earth.
—Genesis 9:13 Berkeley

The "bow in the clouds" is a most beautiful symbol of God's mercy, faithfulness and love. What is more beautiful than a shimmering rainbow after a summer shower? This is a phenomenon no artist can adequately duplicate on canvas, a miracle of color and significance which might be called the smile of God upon men of earth. In our daily lives, we often encounter this rainbow of promise, especially after a storm of trial or temptation. We should be thankful for this token of love and mercy, this covenant of God's faithfulness to us. We should be glad that His faithfulness cannot be measured in human terms, for His is a perfect faithfulness whereas ours is woefully imperfect.

SEPT.
19

But He replied, It has been written, Man shall not live and be upheld and sustained by bread alone, but by every word that comes forth from the mouth of God. —Matthew 4:4 Amplified

There are two reasons why the Bible should be an "open" book to me — that I might be "sustained" or fed by it, my soul nourished; and that I might be "upheld" by it, that it might be a weapon in my hand. If every child of God made this full use of His Word, how much more effective the Church of Jesus Christ would be! Can you say, with the Psalmist, "Thy Word have I hid in my heart, that I might not sin against Thee"? Your testimony and your witness would be so much stronger and so much more effective. To carry on an efficient program of hiding the Word in my heart, I must set aside a definite time each day for dwelling and meditating on this Word.

Jesus turned around and seeing her He said, Take courage, daughter! Your faith has made you well.
—Matthew 9:22 Amplified

Here's another example of great faith. It seems that faith is always the door through which the Lord Jesus walks in performing His miracles — beginning with the miracle of salvation itself and including the miracle of healing. Would this woman have been healed if she had just accidently bumped against the Lord in the press of the crowd? Be careful that your faith rests in the only One with miraculous ability.

Whenever you give . . . do not blow a trumpet before you as the hypocrites . . . do, that they may be recognized and *honored* and *praised by men. . . .*
—Matthew 6:2 Amplified

The word is not "when" but "whenever." It is part of our responsibility; it is expected of us that we will be generous with the means God has given us. Not only are we *expected* to give, we are warned to give, not for the praise of men, but for the glory of God — in secret as far as our intentions are concerned. This means that our motive for giving must be pure, not tainted with any desire for self glory. As soon as we receive glory, we have already received our reward and cannot expect God to reward us further. And think how much greater is God's ability to reward us than is the capacity of man to reward anything we might do. Actually, one is only cheating himself if he desires the praise of men rather than the reward of God — and he cannot expect both.

SEPT.
22
As Jacob looked up, he saw Esau coming. . . .
Esau ran to meet him, threw his arms around him,
fell on his neck and kissed him.
                              —Genesis 33:1, 4 Berkeley

Jacob had been dreading this meeting with his brother Esau, fearing the very worst at the hands of his rough and ready older brother. But he did not only fear this meeting, he also prayed about it. Someone has said, "It is a good thing if our fear leads us to prayer and not to despair." Jacob had asked God to ". . . deliver me, I pray thee, from the hand of my brother . . . for I fear him." Does God hear prayer? Jacob would answer emphatically, "Yes!" Instead of running into a small scale war with Esau's servants, Jacob ran into his brother's arms to be met with affection and tears of joy. As Jacob yielded to God's direction, God worked out the details of his life. So it is with us today, if we are in touch with God through prayer and His Word, if He is first in our lives to go before us.

SEPT.
23
He left nothing undone of all that the Lord com-
manded Moses.   —Joshua 11:15

We often hear how we as Christians should work for our Lord's "Well done, thou good and faithful servant." Joshua knew the secret of earning this commendation for "he left nothing undone of all that the Lord commanded. . . ." Where did he learn what the Lord had commanded? From Moses, God's servant. Where do we today learn what the Lord wants us to do? We also learn from God's servant — but we have, in addition, God's Word itself, which we can approach without an intermediary and which can speak to us without human aid. Notice, too, that Joshua did all that the Lord commanded, revealing not only obedience but also perseverance in the Lord's work.

SEPT.
24
Pray without ceasing.   —I Thessalonians 5:17

Prayer must mean something to us if it is to mean anything to God. If the accustomed time of prayer comes around and we have nothing that interests us enough to pray about definitely and honestly, we would better frankly say so to God than kill time in hollow, heartless formality. To keep up the habit of prayer by saying thoughtless words is not worthwhile. It is a bad habit of prayer, or it is a habit of bad prayer. It is better not to pray than to pray and not be honest. This prayer, however, at least might be always possible: "O God! show me my need of Thee."

— M. D. BABCOCK

SEPT.
25
For with God nothing is ever impossible, and *no word of God shall be without power* or *impossible of fulfillment.*   —Luke 1:37 Amplified

"God specializes in things thought impossible, and He will do what no other friend can do." So goes a popular chorus. What should this mean to me as a young Christian? Should I "run" to God with all kinds of impossible demands, just to see what He will do? Should I boast to my friends that the God of the impossible is at my command? These questions may sound slightly silly, but many people seem to take this attitude toward God. Actually, God's ability to do the impossible should contribute to our awe of Him, rather than our familiarity with Him. Truly, their faith in Him should be limitless because He is limitless — *but* this faith should not be carried to the level of boasting or foolish pride. One of the great impossibles which God has performed was wrapped up in swaddling clothes and laid in a manger. God became a baby so that sinners could become new creatures in Christ.

SEPT.
26
It is God which worketh in you. —Philippians 2:13

This implies the actual presence of God at the center of our being. The very simplicity of these words renders them difficult to understand, for no man understands the complex and marvelous mechanism of his own personality. God works in you — not outside, but in — in the place where thought is born, and the throne of the will is set up, and the affections have their seat; in the inward shrine of the being, God works. — G. CAMPBELL MORGAN

SEPT.
27
And he sat down opposite the treasury and saw . . . the crowd. —Mark 12:41 Amplified

The gospel of Mark is full of intimate glimpses into the lives of real people, a veritable portrait gallery of good and evil. Candidly, Jesus reveals these people for what they are, seeing deep into their lives, analyzing the very thoughts of their minds. Today, He looks as deeply into our lives, seeing the good and the evil in each one. We should be so concerned about spiritual things, that we devote ourselves to Him.

SEPT.
28
The Lord then said . . . stretch out your hand over the sea; divide it. . . . Moses then stretched out his hand . . . and the Lord moved the sea . . . turning the sea into dry land.
—Exodus 14:15,16, 21 Berkeley

Here is a perfect example of what obedience to God can accomplish. If Moses had refused to follow God's directions, God would not have worked on behalf of the children of Israel. God and obedience make an undefeatable combination, just as God and one believer constitutes a majority.

SEPT.
29
Know therefore that the Lord thy God, he is God, the faithful God, which keepeth covenant and mercy with them that love him and keep his commandments to a thousand generations.
—Deuteronomy 7:9

What a marvelous fact to know and to base a life upon! Moses here is reminding the children of Israel concerning God — but the application of these words is much wider than to just these chosen few, for this is the message that has resounded through centuries of time and remains just as true today as when Moses first pronounced its tremendous truth. If we really believed that our God is a faithful God, true to His Word, our lives would be victoriously lived above our circumstances and problems. Our love for Him would be the most important and preeminent thing in our lives. This *faithful* God can deliver us from temptation, He can keep us from falling, He is fully capable of forgiving our sins and granting us victory in Christian life.

SEPT.
30
Ye shall be a peculiar treasure unto me.
—Exodus 19:5

This was the message the Lord commanded Moses to bring to the children of Israel. As God's *peculiar* people, the Israelites enjoyed immeasurable privileges and were assured of divine leadership. Today, the spiritual children of Abraham, the faithful old patriarch from whom the Israelites were descendants, enjoy equal privileges. The Apostle Peter makes this clear when he says, "But you are a chosen race, a royal priesthood, a dedicated nation [God's own purchased, special people] . . ." (I Peter 2:9 Amplified). This is the meaning of "peculiar." Not someone "queer" and different but one who is "purchased" and "special," God's property, living daily for Him.

OCTOBER

**OCT.
1**
Naphtali, a deer let loose; he produces beautiful sayings. —Genesis 49:21 Berkeley

The reputation of Naphtali might well be the desire of every young Christian, for it is apparent from the context that Naphtali's beautiful words came from a beautiful spirit. Words are meaningless unless they are backed up by life, but beautiful words backed up by a beautiful life can be a most effective means of influencing others for Christ. In one of the most familiar Psalms, David pleads, ". . . let the words of my mouth and the meditations of my heart be acceptable in thy sight, O Lord. . . ." He, too, was searching for a beautiful spirit out of which could come beautiful words. That should be our desire.

**OCT.
2**
Whoever desires to be great among you must be your servant, and whoever wishes to be most important and first in rank among you must be the slave of all. —Mark 10:43, 44 Amplified

A rule or motto such as this would be "laughed out of court" by the so-called successful people of today. Greatness in service is a forgotten concept. Today, it is not the one who serves who is considered great, but the one being served. This is even true in the Church of Jesus Christ, sad to say. The one who seems content to serve on the sidelines or in the background is seldom recognized for his contribution to the cause of Christ. On the other hand, the man in the public eye is looked up to as a leader to be followed and emulated. Yet, God's directive for greatness in the Kingdom emphasizes unselfish service.

OCT.
3
These are the legal orders you shall announce to them: . . .
—Exodus 21:1 Berkeley

Chapters 21 through 23 of Exodus might well serve as a textbook for those studying law. Every area of life is taken into consideration in this series of "orders" which the Lord gave Moses to pass along to the children of Israel. These concepts are principles which form the basis for modern legal procedure. Every contingency is considered, for God knows all things from the beginning. This set of standards is completely true, for God is truth. The reason for the breakdown in the system of law today may be traced to the human element of trial and error. If men today would go back to the law as given in the Word of God the confusion would no longer remain in our courts.

OCT.
4
And God remembered. . . .
—Genesis 8:1

This text is made even more meaningful when one remembers that God forgets. Our sins, once they are covered by the blood of Christ, are remembered against us no more. They have been cast into the sea of God's forgetfulness. They have been removed from us "as far as the east is from the west." Yes, we should be thankful for God's forgetfulness, but we should be even more thankful for His remembrance. How do we know that God remembered Noah? For one thing He saved Noah and his family from the flood, just as He saves each of His blood-bought children from the eternal destruction of death. One aspect of His saving power is often forgotten or ignored — the keeping or "on going" power of salvation. He does not remember us today and forget us tomorrow!

OCT.
5

Come thou with us, and we will do thee good.
—Numbers 10:29

Here is a wonderful motto and watchword for the children of God. This word "come" often appears in the Scriptures. God the Father once said (in Isaiah), "Come now, and let us reason together." And God the Son says, "Come unto me all ye that labor and are heavy laden." And God the Holy Spirit (with the bride of Christ) says, "Come." What good can God's child offer to those outside of Christ? The most important is that He can offer the unsaved *eternal* good — eternal life. But it is true, too, that God offers temporal and spiritual good for this life as well.

OCT.
6

Old things are passed away; behold, all things are become new.
—II Corinthians 5:17

A friend of mine was brought up in an Irish coastal town which has a busy little port and fishing fleet. When he was a tiny boy his mother often took him along the seafront, where his special heroes were the coastguards with their big telescopes. His mother bought him a little telescope of his own; then, when the coastguard lifted up his big telescope to look out over the sea, little Arthur would stand by and look through his telescope. One day, as he did this, he piped out, "No ships in sight, Mummie." The coastguard bent down and said, "Little man, look through my telescope." Young Arthur did so, and then, "Ooh, Mummie, ships! . . . ships! . . . everywhere!" The big telescope transformed everything. So it is, but far more so, with us who have become "new creatures" in Christ. We have seen a new world of spiritual realities which we never saw before through our little telescopes of human reason. "All things are become new!"   — J. SIDLOW BAXTER

OCT.
7
Amram married . . . Jochebed. . . .
—Exodus 6:20 Berkeley

In this long genealogy of the sons of Israel, it would be easy to overlook the parents of Moses. They are two of God's faithful servants about whom little is said in the Scriptures. It is their son Moses who gets the limelight as far as the Scripture record is concerned. Perhaps many who read these words are destined never to become "bright lights" in the cause of Christ, but their contribution may be no less significant in the eyes of God than is that of some important and publicized Christian leader. Perhaps you are called to do a "behind-the-scenes" type of service which will bring no recognition from men — but will nonetheless result in God's "Well done, thou good and faithful servant." If we are in the center of God's will, no matter how seemingly unimportant our task may be, we may still take our place in God's hall of fame.

OCT.
8
And when the feast was ended, as they were returning, the boy Jesus remained behind in Jerusalem.
—Luke 2:43 Amplified

Christians often forget in reading their Bibles that the men and women about whom they are reading were "men of like passions," human beings with human failings just as people today. Jesus, too, was a man, tempted as men are today, with this difference — He never succumbed to that temptation. But He could identify Himself with human frailty. He went through all the various stages of growth, from babyhood to adulthood and even spent some time as a teenager. How thankful Christians, particularly young people, should be that He is not an impersonal and disinterested God but one who loved sinners enough to die that a way might be provided for them back to God.

OCT.
9
For what does it profit a man to gain the whole world, and forfeit his life . . . ? —Mark 8:36
—Amplified

How many reading this passage remember the name of the brother of James Hudson Taylor? Probably none of you, but all Christians are familiar with courageous missionary, James Hudson Taylor, who devoted his life to the people of China. Yet, Taylor's brother laughed at James Hudson for throwing his life away on the heathen of China, while he devoted his life to the making of a name for himself as a great doctor in England. Today, no one even knows his name, while the name of James Hudson Taylor still rings and resounds as that of one of God's greatest servants. What kind of a name do you want?

OCT.
10
Be imitators of God — copy Him and *follow His example. . . .* —Ephesians 5:1 Amplified

It is related about a great artist that he was once wandering in the mountains of Switzerland when the police met him and demanded his passport. "I do not have it with me," he replied, "but my name is Doré." "Prove it, if you are," replied the officers, knowing who Doré was, but not believing that this was he. Taking a piece of paper, the artist hastily sketched a group of peasants who were standing near, and did it with such grace and skill that the officials exclaimed, "Enough! you are Doré."

The world cares little for a mere profession. We say we are Christians, but the challenge is, "Prove it." If we are of Christ we must be able to do the work of Christ, to live the life of Christ, to show the spirit of Christ. The artist's skilful drawing proved his identity. We must prove that we are the followers of our Master by the love, the grace, the beauty, the holiness of our life. — J. R. MILLER

**OCT.
11**   *Jethro exclaimed, "Blessed be the Lord who saved
you from Egypt's oppression. . . . Now I recognize
that Jehovah is greater than all the gods. . . ."*
—Exodus 18:10, 11 Berkeley

Those around us who know not God get their concept
of Him from His children. It would be a marvelous thing
if every Christian would so live that others might see and
glorify God in his life as Jethro did in the life of his son-
in-law, Moses. If Moses' life had been full of shortcomings and failures, would Jethro have been as willing to
glorify God? Let each one of us make it our primary aim
to "mirror" God before those around us.

**OCT.
12**   *And when he (Judas) came he went up to Jesus
immediately, and said, Master! Master! and he em-
braced Him and kissed Him fervently.*
—Mark 14:45 Amplified

Probably no more hypocritical act than this betrayal of
Jesus by Judas is recorded in the Word of God. And yet
many Christians today just as blatantly betray their Lord
by their actions. Perhaps it is by denial of Him when
their testimony is "on the line." Perhaps they travel with
the wrong crowd. Or they might betray Him by withholding part of themselves when He demands all of them.
The name of John is the most popular boy's name today
— but Judas is rarely, if ever, bestowed upon a child, merely
because of the connotation of evil which seems to hover
around it. Unfortunately, many of these who are called
"John" are actually "Judas" in their hearts. The prayer
of every Christian should be, "Lead us not into temptation," as the Lord suggests in His model prayer, for every
one of us is susceptible to the subtle promptings of Satan
to betray our Lord as Judas did.

OCT. 13   *Be not afraid to go down to Egypt, for there I will make you a great nation.*

—Genesis 46:3 Berkeley

God's directions are definite and specific. Today, He may not speak directly to His child, as He did to Jacob, but He does just as definitely give guidance to His children. Today, if when the reading of the Word, the events of the day, and the counsel of fellow Christians seem to dovetail together, it means that God has given His "go ahead" to a definite path of procedure for His loved one. Neglect of any one of these areas of the Christian life (especially that of failing to fellowship with God in prayer) will result in an aimless, fruitless life, lived far short of God's best. Remember how God led Jacob, and make it your deepest desire for that same measure of leadership in your own life!

OCT. 14   *And we know that all things work together for good to them that love God.* —Romans 8:28

A farmer allowed his old, worn-out, blind horse to wander about the premises with all freedom. One night the old horse fell into an abandoned well. It was decided that, since the well was useless and the horse was useless, it would be convenient to fill the well and bury the horse with the same operation. But the earth that was shoveled in to cover up the horse, made a good foundation for his feet, and he kept on top of it all the time. When the well was filled to the level of the ground, the old horse walked away to graze on the meadow. This is a parable representing the effect of opposition upon the Christian. "If God be for us, who can be against us?"   — J. B. CHAPMAN

OCT.
15
He threw it on the ground and it became a snake from which Moses fled. —Exodus 4:3 Berkeley

A mere stick was here used of God to teach Moses a vitally important lesson — that "nothing is small if God is in it." If most of us Christians would realize this truth, how much more valuable would our contribution to the cause of Christ become! Humility is fine and a virtue recommended by Christ Himself — but humility is no excuse for cowardice. The Christian who immediately answers, "I can't do that!" when asked to perform a specific task in the church is not speaking from humility as much as he is voicing a fear of the future. Without even consulting his Heavenly Father, he dares to refuse what may well be a directive from the One whom he professes to love and obey. May each one of us Christians be thus obedient.

OCT.
16
Then Satan answered the Lord, "Is it for nothing that Job reveres God? Hast Thou not put a hedge around him. . . ?" —Job 1:9, 10 Berkeley

Why does Satan describe God's protective care around Job as a "hedge"? In the case of the patriarch Abraham, who pioneered for God, and of David, who fought for God, this protective care was described as a "shield." Satan jealously refuses to give God full credit for His greatness in the life of Job. He refuses to honor God's protective care for what it really is. A hedge may surround one who does not want to be "hemmed in." A shield, on the other hand, is a protective covering *used* by the warrior, a voluntary choice of the will. How much more glory for God is involved in the "shield" concept as opposed to the "hedge" concept! God wants to protect the love of His children, but the love must come from the heart, for love that is forced or coerced is not really love but merely fear.

OCT.
17
[For my determined purpose is] that I may know him. . . . —Philippians 3:10 Amplified

Knowing Jesus Christ makes possible heaven upon earth, because no other friend can satisfy like Jesus. The society of the best of earth's friends often grows tedious and becomes boresome. As the wise man of old warned: "Withdraw thy foot (let thy foot be seldom in) thy neighbor's house: lest he be weary of thee and so hate thee" (Proverbs 25:17).

But this can never be so with Jesus Christ! Friendship with Him is an ever new, ever widening and broadening experience, like a superb panorama, with mountains rising higher and higher and with scenic valleys and lovely lakes that uncover endless delights as they are explored.

Christ's friendship is like an inexhaustible fountain of living water. The more we know Him, the more we want to know Him and the more precious He becomes. Unlike some friends, Jesus "wears well." If there is some fault, some failure, some drying up of inspiration in our relationships with Him, we may be sure the fault is never with His side of the friendship. — MERRILL F. UNGER

OCT.
18
Behold, I set before you this day a blessing and a curse. —Deuteronomy 11:26

These were the words of Moses, but the message of them came from the Lord Himself. Life is summed up in this powerful statement — for life can be likened to a fork in the road, one way leading to blessing and the other to a curse. The path of obedience to the will of God is the path of blessing. Disobedience leads to the ultimate end of eternal death. We are faced every day of our lives with this choice. What will your choice be this day?

OCT.
19
Moses . . . paused in the land of Midian, where he sat down by a well. —Exodus 2:15 Berkeley

"Sitting" is often mentioned in the Bible as having much to do with man's spiritual life. David, in Psalm 1, warns against sitting in the "seat of scoffers," and many of God's people made important decisions based on "sitting." Where we sit also determines where we stand. Moses met the daughters of Midian at this well, and one of them became his wife. Our choice of a place to sit and to stand might well be just so decisive. As Christians, we should be vitally concerned that our fellowship be with those of "like precious faith," although our witness must extend beyond.

OCT.
20
And he brought him to Jesus. —John 1:42

Only three things are mentioned about Andrew. He brought his own brother to Jesus (John 1:42); He brought a lad with a simple lunch to Jesus (John 6:8, 9); and He brought the Greeks to Jesus (John 12:22). That is all we know about Andrew. Unnoticed, unappreciated, all but forgotten, but what a ministry was his. Without Andrew there would not have been that great preacher of Pentecost, Peter. Without Andrew the hungry multitude would not have been fed nor the Greeks brought to Christ! Tradition tells us one of these Greeks was Luke, the physician, who wrote the gospel of Luke and the book of Acts. In heaven, Andrew's name will stand high as the man who knew how to bring souls to Christ. You, too, can be a little Andrew. You may not be able to preach, sing, write, or do the "flashy" things that people notice, but you can by prayer and witnessing be a little Andrew. —M. R. DeHaan

OCT. 21

He sent for all the scribes and the wise men of Egypt and Pharaoh told them his dream; but none was able to interpret it. —Genesis 41:8 Berkeley

What a picture of heathendom today, even in so-called Christian America. Those "able to interpret" are rare indeed. And what a challenge this condition should present to Christian young people — to pray, to give, and to go with the wonderful Gospel entrusted to them! Joseph was used of God to interpret Pharaoh's dream and later on to save his brethren, the Israelites, God's chosen people. Each Christian has the potential of service, a potential just as great as his trust in God, a potential limited only by that trust. If every Christian fulfilled his responsibility to witness, what effect would it have on the world around him?

OCT. 22

Peter saith unto them, I go a fishing. —John 21:3

The Church of God has been fishing along the shore. We set our net in a good, calm place and in sight of a fine chapel, and we go down every Sunday to see if the fish have been wise enough to come into our net. We might learn something from that boy with his hook and line. He throws his line from the bridge: but no fish. He sits down on a log: no fish. He stands in the sunlight and casts the line: but no fish. He goes up by the mill-dam, and stands behind the bank, where the fish cannot see him, and he has hardly dropped the hook before the cork goes under. The fish come to him as fast as he can throw them ashore. In other words, in our Christian work, why do we not go where *the fish are?*

— T. DeWitt Talmage

OCT.
23
And He groaned and sighed deeply in His Spirit, and said, Why does this generation seek for a sign?
—Mark 8:12 Amplified

What an indictment of the Pharisees was Jesus' question here given! How much greater an indictment, however, was His groan and sigh in the face of their unbelief and argumentative attitude. Just as we Christians should seek with all our hearts to merit God's "Well done," we should avoid, as if it were a plague itself, destroying Him by "seeking for a sign" when all the sign we need is His accomplished work on the cross and completed plan of salvation. If we truly walk by faith, as we are exhorted to do, we will not need these signs and wonders to reinforce our attitudes and decisions. If God be for us, who can be against us? Let us walk each day in the boldness this concept gives.

OCT.
24
Yet ye have forsaken me and served other gods.
—Judges 10:13

These are the exact words of God to the erring children of Israel and they point out the two-fold nature of sin, a truth which is often overlooked today. Sin is much more than simply forsaking God, for it includes the serving of Satan. There can be no neutral ground, no fence straddling, no taking of "the middle of the road." As Jesus pointed out in the New Testament, a man cannot serve two masters; an individual cannot be truly neutral. He is either "for" or "against." How do you stand? Are you trying to hide behind a so-called "neutral" position? If you are, you are actually serving Satan, the "other gods" of the text. Make the decision today to become a "servant of the most high God" and serve Him with all *your heart and strength.*

OCT.
25
*He looked right and left, and when he saw no-
body, he killed the Egyptian.*
—Exodus 2:12 Berkeley

Notice the one direction in which Moses forgot to look
— up. Do we as Christians often act without looking up?
Do we fail to look for orders from our Commanding Offi-
cer? If we fail in this, we are making just as terrible a
mistake as Moses did, no matter how well meaning our
action might be. "I will look unto the hills, from whence
cometh my help" was one of David's mottoes. We could do
no better than seek this same guidance.

OCT.
26
What agreement hath the temple of God with idols?
—II Corinthians 6:16

You will find that Christianity is pre-eminently practical.
It does not attempt to construct a living society out of dead
matter, neither does it attempt to realize a pure order
among corrupt men, neither does it attempt to give a perfect ethic to paralyzed individuals. It takes hold of the
man first, and remakes him, and then remakes society.
— G. CAMPBELL MORGAN

OCT.
27
*The more they held them down, the faster they
grew.*
—Exodus 1:12 Berkeley

Paradoxical as it may seem, adversity in the Christian
life results in greater fruitfulness. Just as pruning the
fruit tree results in more and better fruit, so, "putting the
pressure on" the Christian should produce better and more
lasting fruit. Water, when heated to become steam, is
much more powerful than in its previous state. Just so,
the Christian under persecution should become more effective in his living and, if need be, even in his dying.

OCT.
28
You also must be ready therefore; for the Son of man is coming at an hour when you do not expect Him. —Matthew 24:44 Amplified

If every Christian took this watchword seriously, what would be the impact of Christians on the world around them? If each one of us would remind ourselves every morning of our lives that "Jesus may come today," what would that do to our way of life? Much of life today seems to be spent aimlessly and without purpose. Time is not recognized for the priceless commodity it is. Every day that passes means one less day of service for the Lord. And yet, many are merely "marking" time, waiting for a better day tomorrow, waiting for a more "convenient season." Let us live each day as if it were truly the day of Christ's return, filling each day not only with service but also with contemplation of the things of God.

OCT.
29
And the Spirit of the Lord will come upon thee, and thou shalt prophesy with them, and shalt be turned into another man. . . . —I Samuel 10:6

Samuel spoke these words to Saul before he became king, foretelling what God would do for Saul through His Spirit. In short, Saul was to be *educated* for his position as king by the Holy Spirit Himself. He was to be fed for his life's work by the Divine Instructor. Saul's only responsibility was obedience to the Spirit that he might be fitted for service. In verse 9 of this same chapter it is said that "God gave him another heart." This is a picture of what God can and does do for His obedient servants today. Have you become "another person" with "another heart," truly having had an experience with Christ?

OCT.
30
A word fitly spoken is like apples of gold in pitchers of silver. —Proverbs 25:11

We live in a din of speech. Words! Words! Words! And many of them are neither gold nor silver. Remember that words have weight to crush, force to drive, sharpness to pierce, brightness to illumine, beauty to delight, consolation to cheer. There are angry words which sow discord and breed bitterness. There are frivolous words which tend to poverty of spirit. There are double-meaning words which are spawned in the atmosphere of hypocrisy. There are icy words which blight like a killing frost. The words which one should school himself to utter are words of refinement seasoned with grace, spoken courteously and in season — words that lift heavy burdens and remain to cheer like the memory of a sweet song. Speak cheerfully and truthfully, thus lifting burdens and glorifying your Father which is in heaven. Pure thoughts and kind words will carry you down the road to beautiful living. —O. G. WILSON

OCT.
31
I wholly followed the Lord my God. —Joshua 14:8

This was Caleb's personal testimony, a testimony that few can give. The remarkable thing is, however, that those around him were able to say the same thing about him — that he wholly followed the Lord God of Israel. Caleb was one whose life stood behind his testimony, whose actions corresponded to his words, whose testimony was convincing because it was a *living* relationship to a living God. Caleb was wholehearted in following his God. We, too, as Christians today, should be able to say with Caleb, "I wholly followed the Lord my God," and then live to back up our statement!

NOVEMBER

NOV.
1
A child left to himself bringeth his mother to shame.
                                        —Proverbs 29:15

Why are rivers always crooked? That I can answer. It is because water always flows downhill and a river just follows the path of least resistance. When it comes to a hill or other firm obstruction, it just goes around it. It follows the downward pull of gravity. Now that is the reason the natural man is crooked — very, very crooked (see Romans 3:9-18, Psalm 14). Until he is regenerated and made alive in Christ, he can only do "what comes naturally." The natural man cannot please God. Human depravity leads down, until overcome by the Power from above by being born again. But even in the believer the "old nature" still pulls down, and it takes spiritual effort to overcome it. This power depends on keeping in touch with God by prayer, Bible study, testimony, fellowship, and obedience to His will and Word. Then the river of your life will cease winding and run straight. Have you prayed today, read your Bible, sought strength to face the current of the world today? Remember, any dead fish can float downstream, but it takes a live and healthy one to ascend the rapids to the fresh headwaters of spiritual victory.

                                        — M. R. DeHaan

NOV.
2
Whosoever will come after me, let him deny himself, and take up his cross, and follow me.
                                        —Mark 8:34

E. Stanley Jones says that the central difficulty in the world today is that we are trying to adjust to one another without any adjustment to God. I know of no other way to adjust to God except along the lines He prescribed. "Whosoever will come after me, let him deny himself, and take up his cross, and follow me."

Once we are adjusted to God through the finished work of Christ, we start living hopeful lives. We get absolutely lofty in our thinking about the beautiful possibilities for men, because for the first time we see what amazing possibilities we have now that we are in the right relationship with the Almighty God.

What's your motive? Why are you doing what you're doing? What is your life all about? If you are a Christian and "dead" to your purely selfish interests, I can rejoice with you that yours is the highest motive there is — to give glory to God in the highest now and forever.

— BETTY CARLSON

NOV. 3
So, we are Christ's ambassadors, God making his appeal as it were through us.
—II Corinthians 5:20 Amplified

In his first epistle to the Corinthians, Paul called Christians co-workers with God. Now he calls Christians Christ's ambassadors. What is an ambassador? He is a messenger. This verse gives the Christian's *authority* for preaching the Gospel. The same verse shows us the source of our *strength* — God Himself. The last part of this same verse tells us what the Christian warrior's message should be — that those now strangers to God might be "reconciled to God." If we take this message, going out in the strength God provides, we cannot fail in our mission as "ambassadors."

NOV.
4

*Beware that thou forget not the Lord thy God . . .
lest when thou hast eaten and are full . . . when
thy herds and flocks multiply and thy silver and
thy gold is multiplied . . . then thy heart be lifted
up, and thou forget the Lord thy God.*

—Deuteronomy 8:11-14

Have you ever had this experience? Have you ever
noticed how in summer a group of trees seems impenetrable?
But, when the winter has taken its toll, one can see beyond the clump of trees to the open country. That's the
way it is with life, too. It sometimes takes the wintry
blasts of difficulty to clear the way so that one can see the
blessings of God in their true perspective. In prosperity
it seems that we become occupied with material things.
In adversity, on the other hand, we see the world around
us as it really is, and we look beyond to the things of God.

NOV.
5

*Casting the whole of your care — all your anxieties,
all your worries, all your concerns, once and for all
— on Him; for He cares for you affectionately, and
cares about you watchfully.* —I Peter 5:7 Amplified

From the writings of Frank W. Boreham comes this
choice bit of philosophy: "I found myself staggering along
under a load that was heavy enough to crush half a dozen
strong men. Out of sheer exhaustion I put it down and
had a good look at it. I found that it was all borrowed.
. . . It was a very stupid but very ancient blunder." Who
has not been guilty of this "stupid blunder," and worn
himself out before the problems had to be met? Worry
about tomorrow is "stewing without doing." It is the mark
of little faith. It is the capital of fear. It is a close ally to
atheism. Worry does not drive away trouble, it only destroys strength.   — OLIVER G. WILSON

I came that they may have and enjoy life. . . .
—John 10:10 Amplified

The difference between an unsaved person, a saved person not living a holy life, and a saved person living a holy life may be illustrated by three rose bushes, viewed first in midwinter and then in June. All of them are leafless, thorny, and seemingly lifeless in winter's frosty sunlight. However, two of them, representing believers, possess life. The third, representing an unsaved person, is dead. It is just as leafless, thorny, and lifeless in June as in January. It is incapable of responding to God's sunlight, warm rains, and caressing dews. Similarly, the unsaved man cannot respond to God's sanctifying power through His Spirit and His Word because like the lifeless rose bush, he is spiritually dead.

On the other hand, the believer who is not living a holy life is like a rose bush, which, when the time of roses has come, produces only leaves and thorns. He has life, but has not responded to the sanctifying influences of God's Spirit and God's Word. The believer who is living a holy life, however, is like a rose plant which, responding to the radiant sunshine and the gentle showers of spring, is covered with a profusion of fragrant buds. — MERRILL F. UNGER

And David went on, and grew great, and the Lord God of hosts was with him.
—II Samuel 5:10

What a testimony to the greatness of God is this flat statement of fact from the biography of David. David "went on" not without having to face difficulties, temptations, and enemies, but always in the path of obedience to God's command. Thus he "grew great." There is no other way to grow but "to grow by going."

NOV.
8

This same Jesus, Who was caught away and lifted up from among you into heaven, will return in [just] the same way in which you saw Him go into heaven. —Acts 1:11 Amplified

Obviously, the people of God can be divided as to their opinion on the *time* of the Lord's return — but there cannot be a division of opinion with regard to the *fact* of His return. The words of the angel as recorded by Luke in our text leave no room for speculation. This announcement is a stated fact, merely serving to underline the Lord's own word as given in John 14:3, where He said, "I will come back again and will take you to Myself. . . ." The early Christians believed God's Word implicitly as they expressed their willingness to "wait for His Son" from heaven, encouraged by the writings of the apostle Paul who promised them that the "Lord himself would descend from heaven" (I Thessalonians). In this hectic day, our concern should be that we are ready for His return.

NOV.
9

Let us not fight against God! —Acts 23:9

The Apostle Paul had a way of stirring up a "hornet's nest" wherever he went, by his outspoken defense of the Christian Gospel. In this instance, a legalistic Pharisee with more than a little common sense sprang to Paul's defense, decrying the attack of his fellows upon Paul's Scriptural position with regard to the Resurrection. It is possible even for dedicated Christians to "fight against God" if they become more greatly concerned about points of doctrine than they are about the souls of men. It is possible for Christians to "fight against God" when they rebel against His revealed will for their lives. It should be our first purpose to harmonize with His plan.

NOV.
10
A continual allowance was granted him by the king, a portion for each day, so long as he lived.
—II Kings 25:30 Berkeley

These words are spoken of Jehoiachin, one of Judah's captive kings, who was granted a daily allowance by a benevolent Babylonian monarch. The words have much greater application to the Christian's relationship to his Lord. In fact, even the unbeliever is granted a daily "allowance" of the grace of God. God's grace is showered in much greater quantity, however, upon the believer. We as Christians enjoy much more than physical blessings from the hand of our Lord. In fact, those who have had deep spiritual experiences have discovered that God's *spiritual* blessings are much more to be desired than are the *physical* blessings He bestows. Here is a marvelous promise almost buried at the end of one of the books in the Old Testament library of history, a promise that we today can rest upon with assurance and comfort.

NOV.
11
It is good for me to draw near to God.
—Psalm 73:28

Our lives are governed by unchangeable laws which we call "natural." One of these laws is that we tend to become like those with whom we associate. This truth should concern us greatly as Christians. Our desire should be to walk daily with our Lord, constantly in tune with His plan for our lives, always facing toward Him so that we might become more like Him by our association. David, the psalmist, realized this and here supplies the secret to victorious living. My close touch with God through His Word, prayer, and meditation will result in a more Christlike walk for me.

*I know in part . . . then I shall know . . . as . . .
I am known.* —I Corinthians 13:12

A class in physics was studying magnets. After a number of experiments, the teacher took several sheets of paper and a box of steel filings. At his bidding the pupils sprinkled the filings on the papers. The fine particles looked like grains of sand that might have fallen from the hand of a heedless child. "Now," said the teacher to one of the boys, "take your paper of filings and place it on the top of that magnet." The boy did so, and there was a sudden stirring among the particles. In a second, the filings had arranged themselves in beautiful symmetrical patterns. Every particle on the paper seemed to have found its proper place. Out of confusion the magnet had brought order. How scattered and jumbled life seems at times! How can we reconcile joy and sorrow, love and hate, life and death? How can there be any plan to things? But a day will come when life will appear to us like filings above a magnet. Then shall we see everything in its proper place making a perfect pattern. — M. R. DeHaan

The eternal God is thy refuge, and underneath are the everlasting arms. —Deuteronomy 33:27

One of the original owners of Mount Morgan, in Queensland, who toiled for years on its barren slopes, eking out a miserable living, never knew that *underfoot* was one of the richest mountains of gold the world has known. Here was wealth, vast, unimagined, yet unrealized, unappropriated. Just so, every believer has, in the wealth of God's promises, a spiritual Mount Morgan under his very feet only waiting to be recognized, claimed, and appropriated.
— Northcote Deck

NOV.
14
For if you believed in and relied on Moses, you would believe in and rely on Me, for he wrote about Me. —John 5:46 Amplified

The remarkable thing about the coming of Christ is not so much that He did come, as the fact that His coming was predicted for so many thousands of years. From the time of Adam in the book of Genesis until the time of the more immediate prophecy of Malachi, a period of roughly more than 4000 years, there is a continuous, positive reference to the coming of this One around whom the entire Bible narrative revolves. There are more than 300 such references in the Old Testament, beginning with God's promise to Eve that her seed would bruise the head of the serpent and cropping up again in Jacob's prophecy to his sons, in Moses' message to the people of Israel, and down through the actual fulfillment in the person of Christ. The whole Bible is full of the Lord Jesus Christ. If He has such an important place in the Word of God, is it any wonder then that He should occupy first place in our lives?

NOV.
15
At all times and for everything giving thanks. . . . —Ephesians 5:20 Amplified

Said the president of a great university, in addressing his students, "Show me the young man who has had failure and has now won his way to success, and I will back him." A man who has never had any failure, whose course has been one of unbroken prosperity, has not the resources of strength and endurance stored away in his life that he has who has suffered defeats and then has risen again and pressed forward to victory. The latter has been growing to manhood while he was suffering earthly defeat. A true man never can be really defeated. He may fail in business, but not in character. — J. R. MILLER

God loveth a cheerful giver. — I Corinthians 9:7

The story is told of a very wealthy man who, upon the occasion of his daughter's marriage, sent a check for $5000.00 to the bridegroom as a wedding present. He sent it by the hand of the bride's sister and when she returned, the man eagerly asked, "What did your new brother-in-law say when you gave him the check?" The girl replied, "He didn't say anything, but when he looked at it he began to cry." "And how long did he cry?" was the question, and she replied, "Oh, I imagine for about a minute." "Only a minute?" roared the disappointed giver. "Why, I cried for an hour after I had signed the check." When we consider how Christ gave Himself for us, it should compel us to lay ourselves and our all at His feet. The secret of the liberality of the Corinthians was this, that they "first gave their own selves to the Lord" (II Corinthians 8:5).

— M. R. DeHaan

Thou hast put gladness in my heart. —Psalm 4:7

How could David make a statement like this? There he was, a fugitive from the revolution generated by his own son, Absalom. Still he could write out of a heart full of gladness, rather than sadness. What was his secret? Simply, God's presence within. David could be driven from his home and his throne, but he could not be driven from his God. Thus, we as Christians need not depend on our outward circumstances for inward peace. Our happiness comes from God "in whom is no variableness neither shadow of turning." David could also say, "Happy is the people whose God is the Lord!"

NOV.
18
His [Asa's] heart was at one with the Lord as long as he lived. —I Kings 15:14 Berkeley

There is no question that it is a great blessing to be the child of godly parents. But that is no prerequisite for godliness, for of his ancestors Asa could say, "Though my father Abijam, and my grandfather, Rehoboam, did evil in the sight of God, by His help I will do right." Asa determined to walk in the way of his forefather David rather than in the ways of his immediate ancestors. Grace is not handed down from father to son; it does not travel via the blood stream. We should be thankful that, whatever our ancestry, we can live in unbroken happy fellowship with our God, after He has given us "the new heart of salvation." Our purpose, too, should be to so live that, were our biography to be written, it could be said of us, as it was of Asa, "Asa's heart was perfect."

NOV.
19
He who lives [in] purity of heart and whose speech is pleasant will have the king as his friend. —Proverbs 22:11 Berkeley

The promises of God are often conditional. One who wants the friendship of the heavenly King must pray as the psalmist did, "Create in me a clean heart, O Lord," before he can take to himself from the Word of God the promise of the Lord Jesus Christ in his Sermon on the Mount: "Blessed are the pure in heart for they shall see God." But this is more than just an *inward* condition, for he who would be a friend of the King must use speech that is "pleasant" or "pleasing" to God. Thus, our inward attitude must be worked "out" if we are to fulfill the conditions of this promise. Once we have fulfilled the conditions, however, we know for a certainty that God will fulfill His promise!

**NOV.
20**

And they were overwhelmingly astonished, saying, He has done everything excellently — commendably and nobly! —Mark 7:37 Amplified

It would be impossible to sum up the earthly ministry of the Lord any more accurately than this. Even His enemies had to concede the goodness of His life. This is the same Christ who "lives in" and indwells the believer. If Christ truly indwells you, your life cannot help but be "commendable" and "noble," for His goodness will be yours!

**NOV.
21**

They continued stedfastly in the apostle's doctrine and fellowship, and in breaking of bread, and in prayers. —Acts 2:42

That is a concise summary of a Christian life. We must not waste time looking for a creed, but accept some things as settled once and for all; we must seek fellowship for what we can give and get; we must attend scrupulously to our spiritual meals; and by these means shall make ourselves strong for intercessory prayer. — J. H. JOWETT

**NOV.
22**

But the soul of my lord shall be bound in the bundle of life with the Lord thy God; and the souls of thy enemies, them shall he sling out. —I Samuel 25:29

These are the recorded words of a wise woman to King David, while he was still fleeing from the hand of Saul. True, David was still hated and pursued, but, despite his circumstances of life, he was perfectly safe in the hands of his God. In the New Testament, Jesus compares saints and sinners to wheat and tares, and promises that when He comes to judge the world, the tares will be bundled up and burned, but the wheat (the saints) will be gathered up and taken to heaven, to be in His presence eternally.

NOV.
23
Wherefore liest thou thus upon thy face?
—Joshua 7:10

There is a time not to pray, a time when prayer can do no more. And that is when it is *time to act.* "Get thee up; wherefore liest thou upon thy face?" was God's command to Joshua when he was praying to Him for guidance and help. What! Not pray? No, not when it is time to act. For as God's intended way of progression for man was walking on two feet, first the one foot, then the other, even so it is in spiritual things. We must ask and then take, ask and then take, and so we shall advance joyfully and continuously in the normal appointed way.

Get up and do! — M. D. BABCOCK

NOV.
24
Do not be afraid . . . I bring you good news of a great joy which will come to all the people.
—Luke 2:10 Amplified

What if the shepherds had not been on duty when the angel came with his celestial announcement? They might have been *asleep* and thus never heard. They might have been *careless* and ignored the angel's announcement. Then too, they might have been *preoccupied* with the world around them and thus overlooked the angel's visit or they might have been *grumbling,* so concerned with their own petty problems that they would not even notice their heavenly visitor. Fortunately for them, they did not fail in their small task, their daily routine, and they were among the first to welcome the Messiah. We, too, must be ever on the alert, no matter how seemingly routine our lives may be, for we never know when we will be entertaining "an angel unawares."

NOV.
25
Watch and pray, that ye enter not into tempta-
tion.
—Matthew 26:41

When you say "Lead us not into temptation," you must in good earnest mean to avoid in your daily conduct those temptations which you have already suffered from. When you say, "Deliver us from evil," you must mean to struggle against that evil in your hearts of which you are conscious and for which you pray to be forgiven. To watch and pray are surely in our power, and by these means we are certain of getting strength. You feel your weakness; you fear to be overcome by temptation — then keep out of the way of it. This is watching. Avoid society which is likely to mislead you; flee from the very shadow of evil; you cannot be too careful; better be a little too strict than a little too easy — it is the safer side. Abstain from reading books which are dangerous to you. Turn from bad thoughts when they arise. — J. H. NEWMAN

NOV.
26
Let the heart of them rejoice that seek the Lord.
—Psalm 105:3

I do not know when I have had happier times in my soul than when I have been sitting at work, with nothing before me but a candle and a white cloth, and hearing no sound but that of my own breath, with God in my soul and heaven in my eye. I rejoice in being exactly what I am, a creature capable of loving God, and who, as long as God lives, must be happy. I get up and look for a while out of the window and gaze at the moon and stars, the work of an almighty hand. I think of the grandeur of the universe, and then I sit down and think myself one of the happiest beings in it.

— *A Poor Methodist Woman, 18th Century*

NOV.
27

I was not disobedient unto the heavenly vision.
—Acts 26:19 Amplified

Solomon epitomized in eight words the history of the fall of the world's great civilizations: "Where there is no vision the people perish." Killed by drudgery — dead monotony. Only vision and imagination can add romance to life and radiance to the countenance. What a man has is dependent largely upon others, but what he is springs from his inner ideals and vision. What a man is, is never the measure of what he may become. What he may become depends upon the inner glow and the ceaseless fire of a great purpose. No one can tell the height to which a man may climb, and no one can measure the depth to which he may descend. The direction he takes and the path he follows will be bounded by the ideals he chooses.
— OLIVER G. WILSON

NOV.
28

Blessed is the man that endureth temptation; for when he hath been approved, he shall receive the crown of life, which the Lord hath promised to them that love him.   —James 1:12 ASV

Let us not be among those who resent temptation. Let us stand with our Lord who willingly met the tempter and resisted him. If we resent temptation, we lose the glory and strength of character that can come only through such testing. "Count it all joy," says the apostle, "when ye fall into divers temptations." He means that by resisting them we grow in grace and in character as we could not grow were our lives set in protected places where temptations could not come. Our temptation is our chance — our chance to win manhood, womanhood, character, and real comradeship with Christ.
— C. C. MORRISON

It is impossible to remember all of them, for they are more numerous than the sands upon the seashore or the stars in boundless space. They are showered upon us daily —morning, noon, and night. As we think of what our gracious God is to us and of what He has done for us, we cannot help exclaiming, "Bless the Lord, O my soul." But while we cannot remember all His benefits, we will remember some. We are reminded of a few in this 103rd Psalm. Many of them begin with the "P." There is: (1) Pardon: "Who forgiveth all thine iniquities." These are not only forgiven, but are forever put away "as far as the east is from the west." (2) Purity: "Who healeth all thy diseases." It was the disease of sin within that brought about our "iniquities," but when God pardons He also heals, puts soundness in the soul, so that we may have power to "sin no more." (3) Preservation: "Who redeemeth thy life from destruction." See also Psalm 121. (4) Parental Protection: "Who crowneth thee with loving-kindness." Many friends can show us kindness, but it is the parent who can show "love and kindness," and our God both loves and pities "like as a father." Then comes (5) Perfect and Perpetual Pleasure: "Who satisfieth thy mouth with good things." These are some of the Lord's benefits, and as we remember them we call upon all within us to bless and praise "His holy name." — JOHN ROBERTS

NOV.
30

He came to Nazareth, where He had been brought up. —Luke 4:16

There are some lessons which we ought to gather from this visit of Jesus to His old home. One is that we ought to seek the salvation of our neighbors and friends, not turning our back upon our old home, though we may have grown great and famous elsewhere. Another is that as young people we ought to live so carefully that when we grow older, we may be able to stand up in the midst of those who have always known us and bear testimony for Christ. There are some good men now whose preaching would have but little effect where they were brought up, because of the way they lived when they were at home in youth. But Jesus' life had been so pure and blameless that He had no need to blush when He looked His old neighbors in the face and began to preach to them. Every young person should so live that he will never be ashamed to hear again of anything he has ever done.

— J. R. MILLER

DECEMBER

**DEC.
1**

Guide and *keep yourself in the love of God.*
—Jude 21 Amplified

If you have ever seen a sunrise or a sunset, you have seen how a glow seems to spread over the landscape, warming and highlighting its beauty. So it is with the love of God as it is shed abroad in our hearts, as God's children. New beauty is given to every area of our lives as this love radiates into every corner. What was once thought impossible or difficult becomes possible and even easy in the light of God's power and purpose. What was once distasteful becomes enjoyable, for, as the Lord said, "If ye keep my commandments ye shall live in my love. . . ."

**DEC.
2**

*Awake, awake; put on thy strength, O Zion. . . .
Shake thyself from the dust; arise.* —Isaiah 52:1, 2

We live in an hour when the foundations of civilization are crumbling, the night of apostasy is deepening, lawlessness runs wild to its awful climax, the powers of anti-Christ increase and abound, and wars and rumors of wars belt the globe. Yet the Church of God, with the only hope and cure for mankind's sin and misery, rests, for the most part, at ease in Zion, and we who claim that Name above every name make mud pies and daisy chains and twiddle our thumbs while a world sweeps over the brink of disaster. We preach a Gospel that is God's dynamite and we live firecracker lives. We sing of showers of blessing and the old-time power and faith, the victory and higher ground, and then we leave it all in the hymn books and go home. — VANCE HAVNER

DEC.
3
My meditation of him shall be sweet.
—Psalm 104:34

The Bible seldom speaks, and certainly never its deepest, sweetest words, to those who always read it in a hurry. Nature can only tell her secrets to such as will sit still in her sacred temple till their eyes lose the glare of earthly glory, and their ears are attuned to her voice. And shall revelation do what nature cannot? Never. The man who shall win the blessedness of hearing her must watch daily at her gates and wait at the posts of her doors. There is no chance for a lad to grow, who only gets an occasional mouthful of food and always swallows that in a hurry!

— F. B. MEYER

DEC.
4
Watch therefore — give strict attention and be cautious and active — for you know neither the day nor the hour when the Son of man will come.
—Matthew 25:13 Amplified

During the last days of His earthly ministry, the Lord Jesus left many last minute warnings and instructions for His followers. One of the most often repeated was, "Watch therefore. . . ." The Lord must have known of the many subtle temptations and spiritually non-essential activities that would plague the path of His children. So it is that He points out emphatically the importance of being ready for the Lord's return at any moment — a return which will be unheralded and with no advance warning. No person, no matter how good a Christian, can be so prepared at all times — without the strengthening and guidance of the Holy Spirit. When Jesus returned to heaven, one of His first acts, apparently, was to send the Holy Spirit to indwell His children for this very purpose of preparing them for His return. Our hearts should be open to His indwelling.

**DEC.
5**   *O send out thy light and thy truth: let them lead
me.*   —Psalm 43:3

There are three ways in which God reveals His will
to us — through the Scriptures, through providential circumstances, and by means of the direct voice of His Holy
Spirit, making impressions upon our hearts and upon our
judgments. The Scriptures come first. If you are in doubt
upon any subject, you must first of all consult the Bible
about it, and see if there is any law there to direct you.
Until you have found and obeyed God's will as it is there
revealed, you must not ask nor expect a separate, direct,
personal revelation. Where our Father has written out for
us a plain direction about anything, He will not, of course,
make an especial revelation to us about that thing. And
if we fail to search out and obey the Scripture rule where
there is one, and look instead for an inward voice, we shall
open ourselves to the deceptions of Satan and shall almost
inevitably get into error. No man, for instance, needs, or
could expect, any direct revelation to tell him not to steal,
because God has already in the Scriptures plainly declared
His will about it.   — H. M. SHUMAN

**DEC.
6**   *There was a man sent from God.*   —John 1:6

Any life is a failure which does not accomplish that
which God sent it into the world to do. We find our work
and our mission by simple obedience to God and submission to Him. He first prepares us for the place He is preparing for us, and then at the right time leads us into it.
We can, indeed, miss our mission in this world, but only
by taking our own way rather than God's. — J. R. MILLER

DEC.
10

I will both lay me down in peace, and sleep: for thou, Lord, only makest me dwell in safety.
—Psalm 4:8

We sleep in peace in the arms of God, when we yield ourselves up to His providence, in a delightful consciousness of His tender mercies; no more restless uncertainties, no more anxious desires, no more impatience at the place we are in; for it is God who has put us there and who holds us in His arms. Can we be unsafe where He has placed us? — Francois de la Mothe Fenelon

One evening when Luther saw a little bird perched on a tree, to roost there for the night, he said, "This little bird has had its supper, and now it is getting ready to go to sleep here, quite secure and content, never troubling itself what its food will be, or where its lodging on the morrow. Like David, it 'abides under the shadow of the Almighty.' It sits on its little twig content, and lets God take care."

DEC.
11

Thou art the Lord the God . . . and hast performed thy words.
—Nehemiah 9:7, 8

Frances Ridley Havergal had a habit of recording instances of God's goodness to her in a record book which she called "a journal of mercies." Therein she recorded promise after promise which God had made and kept. I Kings 8 says, ". . . there hath not failed one word of all his good promise. . . ." What if one word had failed? That would have spoiled the music of God's faithfulness and vitality. But even in one word He has not failed, for "God is love" and "love never faileth." Our all-powerful God is the only One who could live up to such a standard and perform according to words like these!

DEC.
12
*In the beginning [before all time] was the Word
. . . . in Him was Life and the Life was the Light
of men.* —John 1:1, 4 Amplified

What should our Lord's earthly birth mean to me? Just who *was* Jesus and what did His coming mean? First of all, we are told that He was the Word, the Revealer, the very expression of the mind of God. Others had preceded Him telling the Good News, now the Good News itself had arrived on earth. Secondly, in Him was life, the very foundation of life of which He is the Creator. "I am the way, the truth, and the life," said Jesus, and He could truthfully make this statement because He was the foundation of all life, the foundation of foundations! Lastly, He is *Light*. He is the Source of the only true light, not a reflector of it, as we must be once we become His. So, Christ's coming means everything — a firm foundation for life, the source of life itself, and the only revealer of God's tremendous light.

DEC.
13
The Lord our God is one Lord. —Deuteronomy 6:4

God is behind everything, the final, certain One. You cannot analyze, or divide, or explain Him, yet He is the one and only absolute certainty. He is ONE, all-comprehending, indivisible. When you have said that, you have said all. When you have omitted that, you have left everything out and babbled only in chaotic confusion.

— G. CAMPBELL MORGAN

DEC.
14

But his delight is in the law of the Lord; and in his law doth he meditate day and night.
—Psalm 1:2

Meditation upon God's Word is fast becoming a lost art among many Christian people. This holy exercise of pondering over the Word, chewing it as an animal chews its cud to get its sweetness and nutritive virtue into the heart and life, takes time, which ill fits into the speed of our modern age. Today most Christians' devotions are too hurried, their lives too rushed. But holiness and hurry never did suit well together. Prayer and preoccupation have always been strange bedfellows. A head knowledge of the Word may perhaps be consonant with the scurry of the age, but not a deep heart experience of its preciousness. A deep knowledge of spiritual things can only come by the way of unhurried reflection upon God's truth and by prayer. — MERRILL F. UNGER

DEC.
15

And he said unto me, My grace is sufficient for thee; for my power is made perfect in weakness.
—II Corinthians 12:9

It is the essence of our Christian faith that God puts His strength and wisdom at our disposal in times of need. Modern science talks confidently of levels of power that lie deeper than those our normal life is accustomed to draw upon, thus in a way confirming our faith in God's promise. It is a costly error indeed if, in bearing our burden, in solving our problem, or in meeting our temptation, we do not open the way, through prayer, for God's strength to reinforce our human endeavor.

— C. C. MORRISON

DEC.
16
For He stilled the storm. . . , the waves . . . became quiet. —Psalm 107:29 Berkeley

Christ's life outwardly was one of the most troubled lives that was ever lived — tempest and tumult, tumult and tempest, the waves breaking over it all the time till the worn body was laid in the grave. But the inner life was a sea of glass. The great calm was always there. At any moment, you might have gone to Him and found rest.

— HENRY DRUMMOND

DEC.
17
They . . . went everywhere preaching the word. —Acts 8:4

"It was just too good to keep to myself," said a friend to me one day long ago. He had discovered a certain "fishing hole," where the fishing was fantastically good, and he wanted me to enjoy it also. But how loath and slow we are to tell others about the Lord Jesus, which is the best news of all. Truly the joy of salvation is too good to keep to ourselves. — M. R. DEHAAN

DEC.
18
He that winneth souls is wise. —Proverbs 11:30

A person dedicated to Christ is bound to bear fruit. The Bible mentions several spiritual "fruits," but none more often than the positive command of Christ to "go and tell." Every Christian is a witness, and a witness simply tells "what he knows." Since our salvation in Christ is a "know-so" salvation, it is the message of salvation that we are to give out. Beautiful words without personal knowledge to back them up are not "witnessing." If your life doesn't back up what you say, what you say will make no impact on those around you.

DEC.
19

Be filled with the Spirit.   —Ephesians 5:18
Walk in the Spirit.   —Galatians 5:16

God's dynamic to live the Christian life is the indwelling Holy Spirit, whom *every* regenerated soul possesses. The Christian life can only be lived by relying upon the Holy Spirit. The *normal* Christian life is the Spirit-filled life. Unless we as believers are filled with the Spirit, our lives will be shabby, powerless, fruitless, and in a distinct sense subnormal. It becomes at once apparent in the light of this consideration how essential it is to be filled with the Spirit.

But inasmuch as the filling of the Spirit is not an experience to be rested in, but continuously repeated, it is not enough that a believer "be filled with the Spirit." He must likewise "keep filled with the Spirit." Both of these essential ideas are clearly comprehended in the original of Ephesians 5:18, which may more literally be translated, "Keep on being filled with the Spirit." This at one stroke demolishes the widely current mistakes of many of God's dear children in relying upon some past experience of filling, rather than trusting God for a present infilling.

The injunction goes farther, however, than "filling" and "the keeping filled," and involves the actual life of the Spirit-controlled believer. "Walk in the spirit" (Galatians 5:16). A *step* of faith, whereby we claim our birthright of the fulness of the Spirit, must be lengthened into a *walk*.

— MERRILL F. UNGER

Are there not twelve hours in the day?
—John 11:9 Amplified

William Arnot has said, "The very fact of a Christian being here (in the world), and not in heaven is a proof that some work awaits him." Perhaps that is the thought that the Lord had in mind when He asked this blunt question of His disciples. It is challenging as well as rather shocking to realize that the only reason Christians are left in the world is that they might be witnesses to the saving grace of God. And yet we as Christians become so involved in "making a living" and accumulating material blessings, that this primary objective is often shunted into the background and, in fact, completely forgotten in all too many cases. If you are not leaving a Christ-like impression with everyone you meet, socially or in a business way, you are failing to carry out your Christian commission.

Jesus said to them, My food (nourishment) is to do the will (pleasure) of Him Who sent me. . . .
—John 4:34 Amplified

J. Hudson Taylor, the great pioneer missionary to China, once said, "The real secret of an unsatisfied life lies too often in an unsurrendered will." Herein lies the reason why so many people today are discontented and unsatisfied, striving for the unreachable, yearning for the unattainable. Christians, as well as unbelievers, find themselves in this situation. The problem is that they are sacrificing the important on the altar of the immediate, making the tangible of greater value than the intangible. Jesus knew the secret of true contentment, for the most important thing for Him was to do His Father's will. Because He rested securely in that purpose, His life had a serenity that attracted others to Him. That same serenity is available to us.

DEC.
22

Be perfect, be of good comfort.

—II Corinthians 13:11

A glance at the words is enough to make us feel how contradictory they are. *Be perfect* — that is a word that strikes us with despair; at once we feel how far away we are from our own poor ideal, and alas! how much further from God's ideal concerning us. *Be of good comfort* — ah, that is very different! That seems to say, "Do not fret; do not fear. If you are not what you would be, you must be thankful for what you are." Now the question is this — How can these two be reconciled?

It is only the religion of Jesus Christ that reconciles them. He stands in our midst, and with the right hand of His righteousness He points us upward and says, "Be perfect." There is no resting place short of that. Yet with the left hand of His love He holds us close, as He says, "Soul, be of good comfort; for that is what I came to do for thee."

— MARK GUY PEARSE

DEC.
23

Now are ye light in the Lord: walk as children of light.

—Ephesians 5:8

We do not realize the importance of the unconscious part of our life ministry. It goes on continually. In every greeting we give to another on the street, in every moment's conversation, in every letter we write, in every contact with other lives, there is a subtle influence that goes from us that often reaches further, and leaves a deeper impression than the things themselves that we are doing at the time. It is not so much what we *do* in this world as what we *are*, that tells in spiritual results and impressions.

— J. R. MILLER

If we prove faithless, yet will He remain faithful, for He cannot deny His own nature!

—II Timothy 2:13 Norlie's

Here is the secret. Even if we are unfaithful, He remaineth faithful. Do you find that comforting? At this moment God has a message for those of you who have not been faithful to Him. You have been busy building in your life a flimsy sort of structure, pleasant to the eye, easily passed by the superficial examiner, but fundamentally unable to stand the test. But now there has been a storm in your life and all you had built, all you had hoped for, all you planned, has crashed around you in ruin.

You say there is no hope for me! Yes there is. Let this be written across our lives here and now. No matter how unfaithful we are, He — the Lord Jesus Christ — remains faithful. He is constant. He is the same yesterday, today, and for ever. He is the unchangeable Christ.

His faithful promise is contained in many parts of the New Testament. Firstly: "Him that cometh to Me I will in no wise cast out." Remember, He is faithful. He has given an unconditional guarantee that if you will come to Him He will receive you, forgive you all your sin, make you a new creature, and take you into His Kingdom.

Here is the second promise: "If we confess our sins, Jesus is faithful and just to forgive us our sins and to cleanse us from all unrighteousness." No matter what your failure has been, He is faithful, and if you will put your life in His Hands *now* by accepting Him as your Saviour, or dedicating yourself anew to Him, "He remaineth faithful." — ERIC HUTCHINGS

DEC.
25
Mary Magdalene came and told the disciples that she had seen the Lord. —John 20:18

This really is the full Christmas message. It tells not merely of a Saviour born, but also of a Saviour that has lived, obeyed, suffered, died, and risen again, and is able therefore to save unto the uttermost all who come unto God by Him. The shepherds and the Magi found but a little babe when they came to see the new-born King. We see a Saviour with the print of the nails in His hands and feet, who has wrought a full and glorious redemption for the world. Jesus appeared to Mary after He had come again from death; yet death had not extinguished one beam of His brightness. The resurrection was a type and prophecy of the future resurrection of all who believe in Him and sleep in Him. It shows us therefore that death does not mean an experience, and life goes on afterward without loss or marring. We ought to try to learn this blessed truth. Life is not worth living which is bounded by earth's little horizon. Indeed we do not really begin to live until we are living for immortality. — J. R. MILLER

DEC.
26
For it is God which worketh in you both to will and to do of His good pleasure. —Philippians 2:13

As far as we are told in the Bible, the Holy Spirit has no way of getting at the unsaved except through the channel of those who are already saved; He comes to the believer and through the believer convinces the unsaved of sin. What a solemn thought! If we realized that the Holy Spirit could only reach the unbeliever through us, who are already saved, would we not be more careful to present an unchoked channel through which the Spirit of God could work? — R. A. TORREY

DEC.
27
The column of cloud withdrew from the front and stood behind them. —Exodus 14:19 Berkeley

Here is an intriguing thought, almost a paradox. J. R. Miller explained it thus: "It is not always guidance that we most need. Many of our dangers come upon us from behind. . . . assaulting us when we are unaware of their nearness. The tempter is cunning and shrewd. He does not (always) meet us full front. It is a comfort to know that Christ comes behind us when it is there we need the protection." Yes, it is comforting to know that our Guide is also our Protector, that no matter from what direction trouble and temptation comes, our Lord stands firmly between us and it. Our responsibility lies in the realm of being where He can protect us, in the center of His will. Once we step outside of this area of protection, we are on our own. And that is when we get into difficulty!

DEC.
28
Take us the foxes, the little foxes, that spoil the vineyards; for our vineyards are in blossom.
—Song of Solomon 2:15

How numerous the little foxes are! Little compromises with the world; disobedience to the still, small voice in little things; little indulgences of the flesh to the neglect of duty; little strokes of policy; doing evil in little things that good may come; and the beauty, and the fruitfulness of the vine are sacrificed! — J. HUDSON TAYLOR

DEC.
29
And He went up on the hillside, and called to Him (for Himself those) whom He wanted and chose, and they came to Him.—Mark 3:13 Amplified

Jesus is looking for men (and women). As S. D. Gordon has summed it up, "He needs men, He uses men, He chooses the men he uses. *The* qualification He looks for is willingness — strong, earnest, intelligent willingness — to do what He wants done. He takes such men into habitual companionship with Himself." It is this fellowship with the Lord Himself which fits us to be His witnesses and His workers. It is foolish for us to go out to the battle before we are fed by Him to stand fast in the "faith once delivered to the saints." Not only must we be able to stand, but we must be able to move ahead when the opportunity arises and when the will of God is in that direction. Our responsibility is to come to Him — He takes care of the rest!

DEC.
30
. . . as far as . . . the three taverns . . . when Paul saw, he thanked God, and took courage.
—Acts 28:15

Whenever we look back on past blessings and achievements, let it mean instant commitment to a better future. If the mercies of God have been yours, do not build "three tabernacles," that you may abide; but rather, like Paul, call the places where God's mercies meet us "three taverns"; then push on, thank God, and take courage. Every attainment is to be a footing for new attempts, and every goal a point of departure. "A man's reach should exceed his grasp, or what's a heaven for?"   — M. D. BABCOCK

DEC. 31

Watch, therefore — give strict attention, be cautious and active — for you do not know in what kind of day [whether a near or remote one] your Lord is coming. . . . You also must be ready therefore; for the Son of man is coming at an hour when you do not expect Him.

—Matthew 24:42, 44 Amplified

This is the last day of the year — and this warning from the lips of Jesus is a fitting note on which to end our tour of the year. Someone has said, "So live, that when it comes your time to die, you will need not to be ashamed." This might be paraphrased, "So live that when He returns, you will not have to hang your head in shame!" If our every action is governed by this solemn truth — the suddenness of the Lord's return — our lives will truly be Christ-like, our records will be clear testimonies, our futures happy.